CREATING YOUR OWN
WOODSHOP

CHARLES SELF

BETTERWAY BOOKS

Cincinnati, Ohio

DEDICATION

To Frances, for her loving help.

Other fine Betterway Books are available from your local bookstore or direct from the publisher.

00 99 98 97 96   8 7 6 5 4

Library of Congress Cataloging-in-Publication Data

Self, Charles R.
    Creating your own workshop / by Charles Self.
      p.   cm.
   Includes index.
   ISBN 1-55870-326-8 (pb)
    1. Woodwork—Amateurs' manuals. 2. Workshops—Equipment and supplies—
  Amateurs' manuals. 3. Woodworking tools—Amateurs' manuals. I. Title.
TT185.S46   1994
684'.08—dc20   93-48348
                                                     CIP

Edited by Hilary Swinson
Interior design by Brian Roeth
Cover design by Clare Finney
Cover photo by D. Altman Fleischer Photography, with special thanks to woodworker Ken Poirier

Betterway Books are available for sales promotions, premiums and fund-raising use. Special editions or book excerpts can also be created to specification. For details contact: Special Sales Manager, F&W Publications, 1507 Dana Avenue, Cincinnati, Ohio 45207.

ABOUT THE AUTHOR

Charles Self is the author of numerous books and magazine articles ranging from woodworking and home and automobile repair to motorcycle racing and touring. His articles have appeared in publications such as *The Family Handyman*, *Popular Science*, *Popular Mechanics* and *The Homeowner*. He has also worked on projects for companies such as Time-Life, United Gilsonite Labs and Georgia-Pacific.

Other books by Charles Self include:
Backyard Builder's Bible
Bathroom Remodeling
Bricklaying: A Do-It-Yourselfer's Guide
Brickworker's Bible
Building Your Own Home
Chainsaw Use & Repair
The Complete Book of Bathrooms
Joinery: Methods of Fastening Wood
Kitchen Builder's Handbook
Making Birdhouses & Feeders

Making Fancy Birdhouses & Feeders
Making Pet Houses & Other Projects
Movable Storage Projects
101 Quick & Easy Woodworking Projects
Vacation Home Building
Wood Fences & Gates
Woodworker's Source Book
Woodworking Tools & Hardware
Working with Plywood

CONTENTS

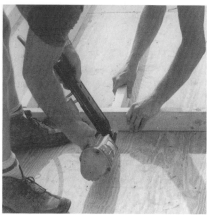

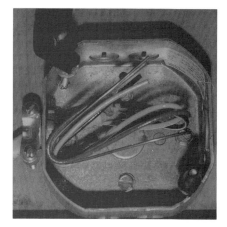

To prevent accidents, keep safety in mind while you work. Use the safety guards installed on power equipment; they are for your protection. When working on power equipment, keep fingers away from saw blades, wear safety goggles to prevent injuries from flying wood chips and sawdust, wear headphones to protect your hearing, and consider installing a dust vacuum to reduce the amount of airborne sawdust in your woodshop. Don't wear loose clothing, such as neckties or shirt with loose sleeves, or jewelry, such as rings, necklaces or bracelets, when working on power equipment, and tie back long hair to prevent it from getting caught in your equipment.

The author and editors who compiled this book have tried to make all the contents as accurate and correct as possible. Plans, illustrations, photographs and text have been carefully checked. All instructions, plans and projects should be carefully read, studied and understood before beginning construction. Due to the variability of local conditions, construction materials, skills levels, etc., neither the author nor Betterway Books assumes any responsibility for any accidents, injuries, damages or other losses incurred resulting from the material presented in this book.

METRIC CONVERSION CHART

TO CONVERT	TO	MULTIPLY BY
Inches	Centimeters	2.54
Centimeters	Inches	0.4
Feet	Centimeters	30.5
Centimeters	Feet	0.03
Yards	Meters	0.9
Meters	Yards	1.1
Sq. Inches	Sq. Centimeters	6.45
Sq. Centimeters	Sq. Inches	0.16
Sq. Feet	Sq. Meters	0.09
Sq. Meters	Sq. Feet	10.8
Sq. Yards	Sq. Meters	0.8
Sq. Meters	Sq. Yards	1.2
Pounds	Kilograms	0.45
Kilograms	Pounds	2.2
Ounces	Grams	28.4
Grams	Ounces	0.04

INTRODUCTION

If any of your workshop areas are like mine, what you have is probably best described as a disorganized mess. You may spend almost as much time cursing the difficulty you have setting up as you do planning and working on projects. In addition to being unproductive, a disorganized shop is a dangerous shop. Stumbling over obstacles is too often the major form of locomotion in amateur woodworking shops. Other shops seem to take on a high sheen of cleanliness that can mean one of two things: Either it's seldom used, or the owner spends most of his or her time cleaning up instead of working on projects.

Unfortunately, small professional shops are sometimes as badly organized as amateur shops. This book will look at examples of both. A large- or moderate-size woodworking operation won't work with the same machinery as you or I do. Handling of materials in an efficient manner — from intake through finish, shipping, dust removal, dust prevention, and safety — are handled differently in different shops. I'd suggest you spend some of your planning time visiting local woodworkers and professional manufacturers. Check the work flow, more than anything else. What we're mainly interested in is the process of getting raw wood in one end and a finished project out the other end, with as much enjoyment and safety as possible.

My main purpose in this book is to let you know how to get the most use from your space and how to increase that space when it becomes necessary. I'll tell you the best site in your shop for various saws, lathes, planers, jointers and other equipment, while considering the amount of working space each major tool requires for safe, efficient operation. Your specific combination of tools, needs and space will determine your particular shop layout and size. Those tool needs vary according to interests. Lathe work, for example, requires a certain amount of space. But if lathe work is all you do, this drops space requirements for other tools considerably. Cabinetry or fur-

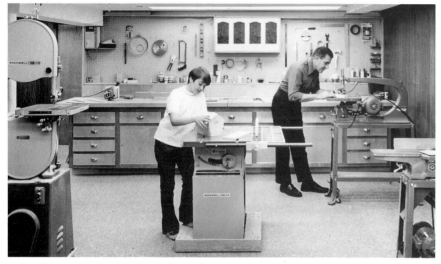

John Capotosto's shop is well equipped today, though probably not as neat and clean as it is in this photograph. John is one of the most experienced do-it-yourself writers in the United States.

Courtesy of John Capotosto.

Dimick Heller's shop is a converted and expanded chicken coop.

niture building can make some major space needs apparent in a rush. Some hobbyists work only with miniatures, decorative inlays, scrolling, band saw work, or hand tool construction of large and small projects. Each requires different tools, different layouts, different expenditures, different planning. For many of us, the new benchtop tools available from most major makers will serve admirably. For others, those tools will give neither the size cuts nor the accuracy of cut needed.

In helping you learn how to make the most of whatever space you now have, we will consider a range of spaces, from the corner of a basement to an entire building. We will even cover the apartment-dwelling woodworker, who faces the biggest challenges. An apartment shop may work if your main interest is with small projects readily done with hand or carving tools or with mostly lathe work. However, be aware that woodworking is a difficult hobby to pursue without a minimum of about $8' \times 8'$ of space, which is unavailable in most apartments. You also need to consider neighbors, who, even at a far distance, will hear the high-pitched whine of power tools. And while the thumps and bumps of hand tools are far quieter, the two types of woodworking often go together.

For a larger shop, a home, rented or owned, might be the answer. Some of the rough plans we set up here require more space than that, including a bit of extra land on which to build. Others present the methods of converting current space to shop uses, always keeping in mind the problems that occur with having a woodworking shop inside your home. For example, I once lived in

An example of Dimick Heller's work that will be for sale at some local craft shows.

This shop is being built by Steve Arrington for one of his clients. It matches the accompanying house, according to deed covenant. It will have a hip roof and brick walls, more than most of us are going to be interested in paying for.

an old farmhouse and used the second living room, or parlor, as a woodworking shop. It made life interesting when it came time to dust and vacuum the rest of the house, and it certainly limited my nighttime pursuit of my hobby.

Woodworking shops serve a wide variety of purposes and suit a wide variety of work. Many people who work with lathes do little else beyond preparing the wood to be turned. They need different tools and layout than do those of us who build furniture or cabinets. Toy builders need smaller amounts of space than do cabinet and furniture makers. Those of us who want to do it all, and who wish to take the work from green, rough wood through finished projects, need more space.

This book also will cover the use of the least-costly materials possible, which may range from light fixtures, to rough-cut wood for framing and sheathing, to siding. With a little effort, you can save a lot of money. For example, I bought my 8′ fluorescent lighting units at a local school sale and spent less than $30 for eight of them. It all adds up to more workshop for less money, with greater safety, efficiency and enjoyment.

I also will show you how to fulfill your needs with what you already may have, how to plan the workshop (often as much fun as using it after everything is completed), and how to set up one of several types of spaces for your own woodworking style, project desires and safety.

Read this book carefully and sort out the tips that are useful to you. You don't need the chapters on framing and flooring and siding if you've got a standing garage to use. You don't need the chapters on cleaning up and setting a basement for shop use if you have no basement.

This book also deals with safety, which is a point not made often enough. We must keep in mind that while power woodworking tools are far more dangerous than hand tools, hand tools can be extremely hazardous. One of my worst injuries while woodworking was when I got impa-

Freddy Reburn's shop is in his basement, where he turns out many fine projects, such as these locomotives. Freddy is retired from Norfolk & Southern Railways.

tient in completing a project, rushed, slipped and jammed a chisel into my left hand. And this happened recently! The bone-deep cut took weeks to heal. The chisel was razor-sharp, as it should be, but I wasn't. All I needed to do was slow down and think. I didn't and suffered an injury I'll remember for many years. This just reinforces an old lesson: Attitude plays a major part in woodworking. Think safe, and you are on the path to working safe.

I can't change your attitude, but I can recommend shop layouts that my experience, and that of other experts, show to be the safest. If you approach any of these plans with the right attitude, you can certainly make your shop as safe as it can be. Remember, you are responsible for your own safety and the safety of others in your shop. If something I recommend, or present as recommended by others, doesn't seem safe to you, regardless of your level of experience, do *not* follow that recommendation. Work out

a different way of doing things.

We live in an era when hobby and small production woodworking shops may be equipped with not only more tools than ever before, but with tools that are easier to use and produce more accurate results than ever before. In some senses, this is the golden age of woodworking tools: Quality tools are accessible and affordable for the average person. The concept of hand-made tools and projects is superb, although the great wood furniture producers of the past had a slew of apprentices to do the grunt work. Today we use machines. We can do the work in the same manner as our forebears did. There is no reason not to do so if we enjoy that kind of work. At the same time, it is a simple matter to produce work that appears the same when finished but is produced with far less effort—though it probably takes just as much thought. Dovetail joints can be hand-cut, taking time and patience, or they can be machined with a router and a dovetail jig. The end result is the same. Today the amateur woodworker can equip a shop with power tools that can give results of a master craftsman. In the process, a lot of useful items get made, and a lot of fun is had.

Most of the information in this book is on power tool woodworking, which is where most of my experience is. Most woodworkers today are interested in getting the best use from their power tools. Hand work is a great deal of fun, and very interesting, but it's not that popular for all facets of woodworking.

With this book I have gathered my experience and knowledge of woodshops and shop construction and tried to present this information in a useful and helpful way. I have also consulted the advice and wisdom of countless other woodworkers on shops and remodeling methods. I have visited many shops with many different layouts. If you want complete information on laying out a shop, it is here. If you want a recommendation as to exactly what tools your shop should have, you will miss the point. Those recommendations are impossible. Although I've described the major power tools for today's shops, I don't work as you do, and you don't work as I do. And that's as it should be. Pick and choose and set up your own shop as it suits your needs and desires.

You will find a few projects in this book, primarily for space-saving designs for workbenches and shelving. This is much more of a planning book than a project book. If you are an apartment-dweller, you are limited in tool use because of space limitations. I have taken that into account. A small woodworking shop area is what you need to construct in the way of a shop. Add your tools and a shop vacuum, and go to work.

Enjoy the planning stage of your new woodworking shop. New is always fun, and if you've carefully planned for efficiency, fun and safety, the result will be a fun, safe and efficient shop.

I've immensely enjoyed doing the book. I hope you get enjoyment and value from my efforts.

CHAPTER 1

DEFINING YOUR WOODSHOP NEEDS

To start, you must look at your workshop needs and methods of defining those needs. This is an essential step toward determining the best layout requirements for your shop, within limits of available space and cash. While one person may be satisfied with a simple layout where the primary tool is a table or radial arm saw, others desire a lathe, band saw, scroll saw or other stationary tools. Your individual needs will differ depending on how you work. The differences are wide, with some people moving from saw to lathe to finish, and others moving from saw to jointer to assembly to finish. These will vary with project requirements and personal needs. The concept of handling wood doesn't change, regardless of the machine size. The variables of interest are size and efficiency in methods and speed of handling material at any particular point in the production process, whether the woodworker is amateur or professional. We will look at what others do to increase efficiency and safety of handling various types and sizes of materials, because their steps can often be adapted to our own uses.

The primary purpose of any woodworking shop is to have raw material—wood—come in one end and a finished product move out the other end. Those ends may be only a couple of feet apart, but the process works better if there is a distinct setting for the varied operations, from wood storage, to working up rough wood, to cutting wood to size, to assembly, sanding and finishing. Most of us must combine the different processes. An ideal shop might begin with a planer, backed by a door, or even a double door, with the table saw next in line. Next to the table saw will be the jointer, and just past those two might be a workbench for test assembly and general hand woodworking. The bandsaw might be near this bench, as might the drill press. Other major power tools, such as scroll saws, sanders, lathes and radial arm saws, are placed where work flow to and from them is most efficient and safest. In a single-person shop, work flow safety should never be a problem. However, if you have people who occasionally work with you in the shop, it may become one. Keep that in mind as you plan.

Design for shops is far simpler if you know what kind of work you wish to do. Simple woodworking gets very complex when all varieties are considered. Well-designed shops work well for a great variety of wood-shaping activities. You need to plan for and design for your machinery and tools to be arranged to do the chores you find most important in the order you find most important.

A small power woodworking shop may have only a single stationary tool—either a bandsaw, radial arm saw or table saw—but it is far more likely that one of those basic saws will be combined with a jointer or a scroll

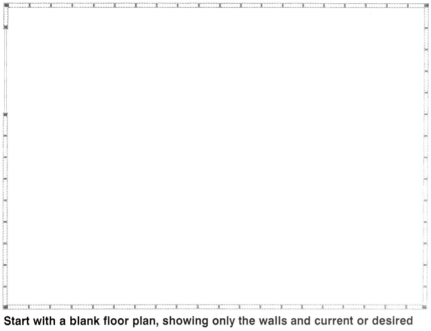

Start with a blank floor plan, showing only the walls and current or desired measurements, and make scale cut-outs of your tools to create your dream shop.

or bandsaw. With this kind of basic setup, it's possible to do most kinds of woodworking. You can make everything from simple boxes to extremely complex projects of varied shapes in surprisingly small woodshops. (In chapter three, we'll look at the tools and the jobs they do to help us determine just what we need to plan for.)

Here, you need to decide what kind of woodworking you wish to do and how it fits in with space needs and possibilities. If you have yard room to construct a freestanding shop, your freedom of choice in various woodworking areas is obviously a lot greater than it is if you must use part of a basement. Better than a basement shop is a garage, either attached or freestanding.

The projects in this book will help make the shop more productive. I won't spend a lot of time telling you to save old coffee cans, icing containers, nut containers or detergent bot-

tles. You probably already know this. This book is concerned with helping you design and build your shop.

USING YOUR AVAILABLE SPACE

Your objective is to take the space you have available and arrange machinery and benches to give the best woodworking efficiency for your particular form of woodworking without spending any more money than is essential. To do this, we look at the amount of space needed to work with a tool and the space required to work tools in conjunction with one another.

Planers and table saws should be placed close to the entry areas of a shop, while lathes and drill presses can be placed in corners. You may want to change the order of placement depending on your personal needs. I recommend the table be placed close to the shop's entry; you may need it to rip boards to width

for feeding through the planer. Next in line is the jointer. And so on, to a wide array of others, including benches.

A small shop doesn't always need to be super-efficient, and a large one isn't automatically efficient. You must take into consideration desires and needs during planning.

Each of us planning a workshop has different desires, different working methods and different needs. A table performs certain jobs and requires space of a particular shape and a particular type of lighting to suit those jobs. The order in which you do the jobs and how you combine them with other jobs done by other tools at other times is what gives your work its individuality. The table saw needs space in front and behind for rip cuts of the lengths you are most likely to require and space for grooving and molding operations. The table saw also requires space at one or both ends for cutting off long panels or boards. The length of that space depends on the size of materials you plan to work with.

If you lay out space for a shop and leave the same size and shape of space for each tool, you'll either reduce the efficiency (and safety) of the tools, or waste a lot of floor area. A drill press or band saw doesn't normally require the amount of working space that you need for a table saw, radial arm saw, jointer or planer.

Tools You Will Need

One of the first chores of shop design is to decide which tools you feel you must have to start. These may be tools you already have on hand, tools you plan to buy in the future, or tools you only wish to own. Decide on the areas of woodworking that interest

***Delta's Unisaw* is one of the classic light production saws. It is exceptionally accurate and powerful.**

Courtesy of Delta.

you most and aim for a shop that suits those needs. If you need more space or a different design for later, you can start with your current layout as a basis and adapt your shop to your changing needs. Attempting to build a shop to suit everything you *think* you will want can be expensive even without buying the tools to complete filling the space.

Designing and building to suit actual needs is cheaper and easier than trying to build a shop for the future. One of the problems with working up a shop design is the amount of time you can waste doing designs that are nothing more than "blue sky" designs that will never be used. Be practical. I've got a disk load of designs that are too extensive to be affordable.

Over the years, I've had a wide range of home shops. I've used a platform of plywood laid on two 2″ × 4″s over two sawhorses and set in the yard with a 10-gauge extension cord. I have also had an 18½′ × 63′ basement shop that was exceptionally handy, but it was hard to keep clean and hard to move tools and materials into and projects out of. The exterior doors were set at a 90-degree angle to the interior doors, with the exterior door height being under 6′ and the doors' width almost 8′. I've used a parlor in a country home and a portion of an oversized office room in another large rented house. I've used a collapsible bench as a workbench in the yard, the dining room and a hall. I've used a multipurpose tool attached to a large drum dust collector in an unused dining room area.

FREESTANDING SHOPS

A freestanding shop is the ideal shop. I am currently happy to be constructing one, after having shops in the small places that I just described. I hope my new shop will serve the rest of my working life and on into retirement. By describing the construction of my shop, I will show you some techniques that may be of use to you also.

The shop will be 24′ × 48′ and two stories high. The office, a darkroom and storage will occupy the second story.

My new shop will have a bottom floor that is pole construction, with the second story in platform framing. The poles (which may be inexpensive used telephone poles) will be on 8′ centers and the studs upstairs on 2′ centers. The upstairs will have a free span for the entire office. I'll use trusses for the rafters. The inside shop walls will be placed on 2′ centered nailers running vertically, giving a thick wall; I'll sacrifice some space, but it will save me a great deal of money in frame. The nailers will be 2″ rough-cut Southern pine.

I'll need three rows of poles because I don't want to use trussed joists; they're too costly for this project when I can lay in 2″ × 10″s for next to nothing. For a few dollars more, I can square up the interior and exterior, which will save me a great deal of trouble. The interior is easily done, but the exterior will require a great deal of shimming and luck. One of my neighbors built a pole shop some years ago and his biggest problem has been getting anything on the inside square since then.

Electrical requirements are something to consider while planning your woodshop. I will have 200-ampere service. This will enable me to run all the tool circuits on ground fault circuit interrupters. Each floor will have

a minimum of two lighting circuits. While this isn't code required for the square footage of the building, it's a personal preference because it means a tripped breaker doesn't leave you completely in the dark. One bank of lights should always work. (More detail on electrical wiring and lighting is supplied in chapter four, covering absolute and theoretical electrical needs for freestanding and other shops. There's also some information on doing the wiring yourself. Always check your local code requirements.)

A workbench I built for my last shop.

The parlor workshop I had some years ago was dominated by this pegboard placed over a workbench. Pegboard makes for great tool storage in a small space.

At the outset, my shop walls and most of the office walls will be open studs or nailers. As time passes I'll put up ¼″ waferboard, pegboard and similar materials to provide an enclosed space. I'll also insulate behind the interior walls using 3½″ of fiberglass. Exterior walls probably will be 1″ × 6″ rough Southern pine placed as clapboard, although I'm also thinking of 1″ × 8″ pine run vertically with 2½″ battens.

The shop floor will be wood. I do not care for concrete shop floors for a couple of reasons. First, they're rough on the feet, ankles and lower legs after a few hours. (Regardless of the type of floor you have, plan on having an antifatigue mat near your workbench.) Second, they're rough on any edged tool that gets dropped. Drop a new plane on a concrete floor and the odds are excellent it will be ruined. Drop the same plane on a wood floor and it usually will be fine. But concrete fits well with pole construction and usually costs less than low-level floor framing, where joists and beams must be of pressure treated wood. However, my shop is on uneven ground where fill and general work-up for a concrete floor would add considerably to costs. An actual framed wood floor is cheaper. If you must go with concrete, you may be able to afford to put in sleepers and ¾″ tongue-and-groove plywood.

My second story floor will be 1″ poplar subflooring at a 45-degree angle to the joists, covered by ⅝″ tongue-and-groove sanded plywood that will get a few coats of polyurethane. It should require no care beyond vacuuming and mopping up spilled coffee.

Windows on the ground floor will

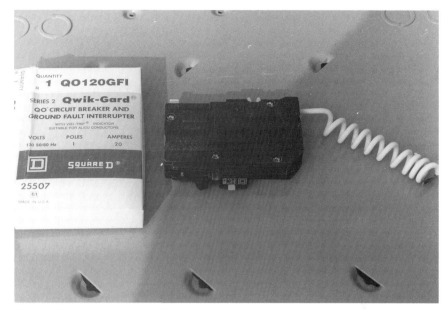

Ground fault interrupters (GFIs) are not code required, but they may save your life. I recommend them for all tool circuits.

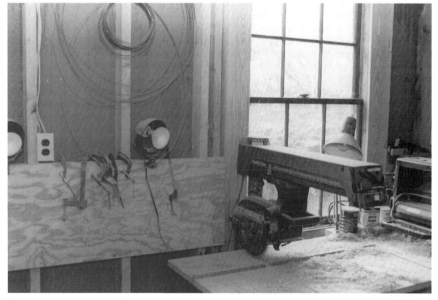

This shows the usefulness of open wall studs as storage for some types of clamps and lights.

be few and start at least 4½′ from the floor so that I can place tools where I want without restriction from glass. It has been my experience that natural light in a shop is highly overrated. It always seems to be either too dim for sensible use or too glaring to be any good. I have a friend who placed his windows at a fairly normal

residential height, about 34″ from the floor to the sill, limiting workbench height and tool placement. He ignores the windows and places his tools in front of them anyway. The windows are constantly dirty, diffusing the light. This is a no-win situation, so try to avoid it. My friend also regrets having used so many windows in his 24′ × 40′ shop. He's got nine—four in each side wall and one in an end wall. He also has two single doors 36″ wide and a double door 6′ wide, which all adds up to a lot of lost wall space. When he first moved into the shop he felt he had space enough for anything. Woodworking doesn't work that way. Sooner or later even the largest affordable shop has its walls hung with clamps and hand tools and templates and patterns and heaven-only-knows-what-else. You need to make allowances for the increase in tool numbers, jigs, templates, patterns and other wall-hung items that are sure to come along.

Consider the way the sun rises and falls in your area. At one point during the day the light will be perfect through most windows. The rest of the time it will be glaring in your eyes or will be so dim you have to bring over an individual project light if you don't have enough ceiling lights. I'd prefer placing enough windows for ventilation only and letting the local power company provide 99.9 percent of my light. If I can work the design properly, I plan to construct 6′- to 8′-wide, inward-swinging, awning-style windows. They'll open from the bottom and pivot at the top and will be hauled to the ceiling on a rope and pulley setup I've only got mentally worked out. The entire outside of the window will be screen, and I may set fans in more than one. Another option is to set whole-house fans in the walls with automatic opening vents—when the fans go on, the vents open—but that tends to be costly. I can build the pivoting windows in the shop as it is constructed. The windows will be easy to make out of decent pine, acrylic plastic ⅛″

or ³⁄₁₆″ thick, and some screening. Add a few hinges, a pulley per window, some chain or rope, and a bit of paint, and they're all done. Placed no lower than 6′ from the floor, these windows should eliminate glare while allowing any available breeze to clip through and take away the heat that collects high in the shop.

Freestanding shops can be equipped with garage doors, which help prevent the nightmare of making a project too large to get out of your shop. The new types of garage door openers are truly a welcome addition. The back strain saved is well worth the cost and the work of installation. Pick a brand designed for easy do-it-yourself installation.

Freestanding shops are the best for getting a good finish on your projects because there's less likelihood of household activities raising dust to settle on a damp finish. You can store all your finishing equipment there. While sawdust can create problems when finishing, you should clean up and cover up after using the equipment and wait for each project to dry. Ventilation of finish odors is less of a problem in a freestanding shop because you can install an exhaust fan and get rid of most of the smelly fumes, but you don't have to worry about those fumes getting into living areas. I suggest, strongly, the use of high-volume, low-pressure spraying equipment, or top-quality nylon bristle brushes, and water-based polyurethanes for most finishing jobs today. If you insist on having volatile solvent-based finishes, you need a spark-free fan and good ventilation.

BASEMENT SHOPS

Basements can make great shops, but there are disadvantages to them. If

you plan to use a basement area for a shop, keep in mind height considerations. The biggest drawback I put on working in basement shops is the sudden stop you get when swinging a board into place, only to be stopped by the floor joists above. Other disadvantages include excess dampness, lack of ventilation, dust, noise, and difficulty in keeping unauthorized people out of the shop area.

Remember that your light from outside a basement will be minimal, so plan lighting accordingly. Basements should also have some kind of outside opening for ventilation. When selecting basement areas to clean up for shop installation, windows are a nice extra, but they aren't essential. If you have them, try to use them for ventilation only.

Dampness can be dealt with by using a dehumidifier. Air conditioning will help in the summer months. The limited overhead room is something you just have to adjust to, by working with small projects or being extra careful with the long wood you need for larger projects.

Some basements are equipped with exterior entry doors. With most modern homes, that's not the case. I have replaced the 30″ exit door in my basement with a 36″ door, but even that is a minimal access size for a woodworking shop. If the only door to a shop is a single door, it needs to be 42″ wide to allow decent movement in and out of materials and projects. You're still limited in project size, but not quite so badly as with a 32″ or 36″ door, which are common entry door sizes. You may want to consider installing a double door to your basement shop.

Use as much of the basement as possible for your shop, and make cer-

Wooden Boat's shop has many windows and uses mostly overhead incandescent lighting.

tain that there is a good door between the shop and the furnace, with any air transfer going through filters. Do the same for any parts of the basement that are finished and not part of the shop. Use good, tight-fitting doors, and keep them closed to help keep the dust down.

A good dust collection system is essential to a basement shop, probably more important than in a well-ventilated freestanding or garage shop. This is key. If there is any doubt in your mind about keeping dust out of your lungs, *wear a mask*. Masks, goggles, face shields and similar items are uncomfortable and sometimes difficult to work in, but I wear them unless I'm working out-

Dust collectors on radial arm saws are helpful.

doors on a windy day. I wear my safety glasses all the time, and they have saved an eye for me numerous times.

In my younger days, I was the dust collection system, with my trusty push broom and a bunch of burlap sacks. The factory got cleaned up nightly, and I was the one doing it. No one took notice of the fact that a kid learning to work around the shop was choking on dust. Everyone else was choking on dust too when I swept and bagged the sawdust and shavings. Luckily, I don't seem to have as many ill effects from that experience as one might expect, but eventually it could all catch up. Spare yourself the possibility.

Finishing areas in basement shops must be ventilated to the outdoors and also need to be isolated from the remainder of the house. A friend of mine, whose small and lovingly worked-up basement shop appears several times in these pages, uses mineral spirit finishes, but he moves from the basement to the garage to do his finishing. Although it's not always possible, it's a good idea to consider moving the finishing operation out of the house. It gets rid of odor problems and any problems with flammability. Water-based finishes can help alleviate ventilation problems, as well. And some new products are on the market that are safer for us and the environment; you should look into those.

GARAGE SHOPS

The garage is the first place people usually think of when planning a shop. If your planning can include space in a garage, you're in good company. My father was an auto mechanic, and I was probably sixteen

years old before I knew home garages were mainly for holding cars. Tools, workbenches and projects seemed to fill our garage.

Garages can lend themselves to large shops or smaller, expandable setups that come into their own with the family vehicle(s) backed into the drive and the tools pulled away from the walls. Garages are good settings for mobile tools and multipurpose tools, because the tools can be pulled out, creating enough space to work. Multipurpose tools like the *Shopsmith* and *Total Shop* are great alternatives for those woodworkers who have a minimum of space to work with. Multipurpose tools are machines that accept accessories for all facets of woodworking. The *Shopsmith*, for example, is a table saw, lathe, horizontal boring machine, drill press and 10″ disc sander, with a plethora of available accessories and attachments that add belt-sanding, band-sawing, scroll-sawing, planing and other applications. You might not need all those tools, but even a table saw and a drill press tend to use lots of space, with those two tools alone taking about the same square footage of the *Shopsmith*. (There are pros and cons for multipurpose tools, which I will discuss in greater length in chapter three.)

If you have a multipurpose tool like a *Shopsmith*, for example, it can go against the back wall and take little more space than 6′ in length and 2′ in width. Even old garages will accept the family car with that little interference. You then can back the vehicle out, pull the tool out and go to work. When the job is done, fold it up and roll it back into the wall space. The same process works with individual power tools on wheels,

I still make major use of this dust collection system—but now, I use a dust mask.

mobile bases or shop-made stands.

Garages are among the easiest conversions for shops. In most cases, you can lay out a large shop in a 24′ × 24′ building. If there is no need to keep vehicles in a garage, you're well on your way. If half has to be saved for the vehicle, you've still got a decent-sized shop, at about 12′ × 24′. You can design your shop to accommodate vehicles when there is rough weather.

SHOPS IN MINIMAL SPACE

Even apartment dwellers can enjoy many phases of woodworking. Some tools are relatively small; band saws and scroll saws, for example, can be readily stored in a closet. Such tools also are quiet enough for an apart-

Shopsmith's Mark V, and other multi-purpose tools like it, provide a complete woodshop in a very small space.
Courtesy of Shopsmith, Inc.

ment setting. A collapsible bench like the *WorkMate* makes a great storable workbench, with accessories that let you do many different kinds of holding (clamping) jobs. In a small apartment setup, finishing will be a problem. But with a little creativity, you can overcome this. Consider finishing outside or near a window with a fan. Use your tools with vacuum dust collectors. Creativity is the key when developing a minishop. Sanding dust is always with us, but new technology has brought us finish sanders with vacuum attachments. I just got a new random orbit sander, the best type of sander for all-around use, which takes a long hose that then goes back to fit any 1¼″ vacuum hose. It works nicely because the prepunched sanding discs allow dust to be drawn through the sander, into the vacuum. You can purchase small shop vacuums that will work nicely in a small shop. Sanding dust will ruin a home vacuum in short order.

The *WorkMate 300*, one of the collapsible workbenches.

FINISHING AREAS

Finishing areas present issues of both safety and quality in the woodshop, whether amateur or professional. Dust in the air will ruin the finish of projects. One of the signs of a poor finish job is a rough, bubbled finish, and that can be prevented. It's more a sign of rush than of anything else. As amateurs, we've got an advantage: We can shut down all other operations when finishing. Shut down long enough for the dust to settle, and make sure the project surface is clean and free of grease as well as dust. Use a tack rag, after letting the shop air settle for at least four hours, and you'll save a lot of grief over failed finishes.

Arrange ventilation to clear fumes quickly. A spark-free fan works best, or use nonvolatile finishes. Always use a good mask or respirator.

Although it is difficult to afford both the space for a finishing area and a method of closing off the dust from the rest of the shop, you should not let space and financial restrictions stop you from working with wood. It's fun. It's relaxing. It can even be profitable. It requires as much space as you can afford to give it, from a patch no more than about $3' \times 6'$ in an apartment to as large as you can afford to construct and fill with tools and materials.

PLANNING AND DRAWING

Settle back and plan. Then settle back and plan some more. There are even programs for your computer that you can use for this purpose. You can use a computer-aided design, or CAD, program to do floor layouts of your available space and

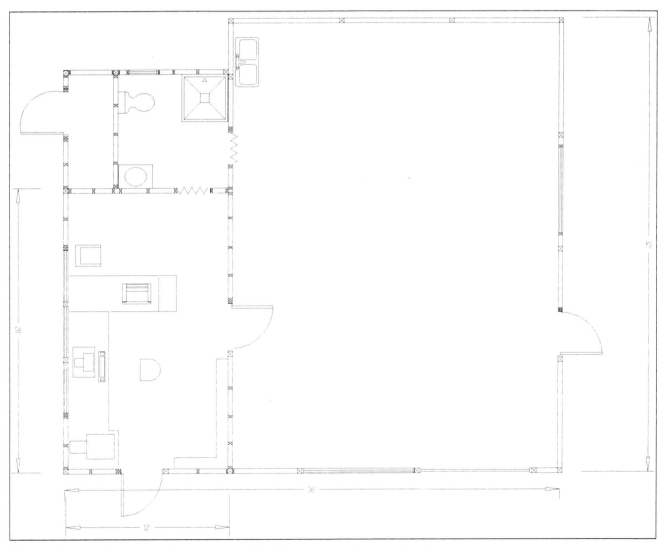

This workshop/office design is based on a 32' × 36' pattern, with a shed roof over the office side and 24' trusses over the shop.

your intended construction. I've included a couple of mine, and I hope they'll give you an idea or two. You can also use graph paper if you don't have a computer, or just do a rough drawing on a sketch pad.

With a computer and a CAD program, your drawings will be more easily changed, but some drafting programs are difficult to use. There are programs specifically designed for the shop planner. I use one called *Generic CAD6*, by *AutoDesk*, who also has a simple, less expensive drafting program called *AutoSketch*. I also have used the *Windows* version of *Auto-Sketch*. This is fairly simple to use to get things down on paper. The tutorial is one of the best for floor plans and dimensioning, and the symbols

pop into place more easily than in any other program I've used. There are simpler programs on the market, but if you have a lot of odd angles in your drawings, those aren't always the best.

I also have used *Foremost's Drafix for Windows*, and found that far easier to use than any other full-load drafting program I've tried. It helps that I've been using the basic *Drafix* program for some years and the power of the *Windows* version is great and easy to use with the *Windows* interface.

A drawing program is not essential to planning your shop. You can simply lay out your dimensions on a sheet of graph paper and make scale drawings of the tools and work areas

such as benches. Arrange these for optimum efficiency. Follow local codes. What's important is to get a layout going, make it practical, and understand what you want, what you will get, and how you'll go about getting there. Whether you use graph paper, a ruler and a pencil, or the most sophisticated drawing program is only relevant as long as you realize each is just a tool to help you plan your shop.

Planning is the most important step in getting a productive shop. Start by listing the tools you want in your shop and those you have. Make your choice of shop type from the realistic options available to you, and define what projects you think you will want to make. Then choose your

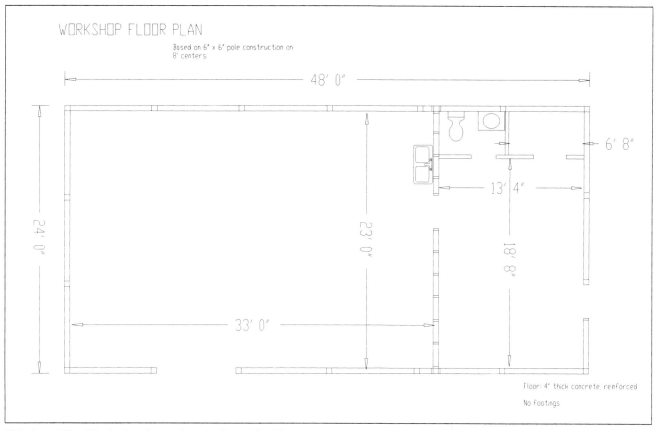

This is a 24′ × 48′ design for a shop built on 6″ × 6″ posts.

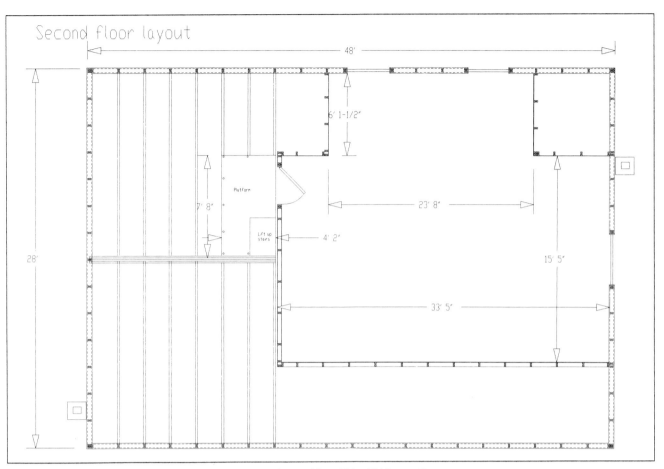

Second floor layout

A pattern for my second floor office built over a shop with a 28′ × 48′ base. It would have proved far too costly although the size is still tempting.

tools and accessories to fit your space and projects.

It is important to define your desires and know what your restrictions are. If you live on a 100′ × 75′ lot and have a 65′ × 24′ house and a 16′ × 32′ swimming pool already in place, don't expect to fit in a 24′ × 44′ freestanding woodshop as well! If you live in an apartment, don't expect to move in a 500-pound saw and a 15″ planer. Remember, it is a lot faster, easier and cheaper to make changes in drawings than it is to change the physical structure if you have made a mistake. If changes to a garage or basement are extensive, you may need some kind of drawings

for your local building department. If you're going to erect a freestanding shop it is almost inevitable that you have some kind of plans drawn up for the local government before it will issue a building permit. Keep in touch with your local building department. Their codes are based on sensible construction methods and are aimed at making buildings safe to occupy and use. Building codes vary greatly, as do inspection requirements. Some parts of Maine, for example, do not require building permits for decks and porches, while areas in my home state of Virginia do. Again, check with your local government for code requirements.

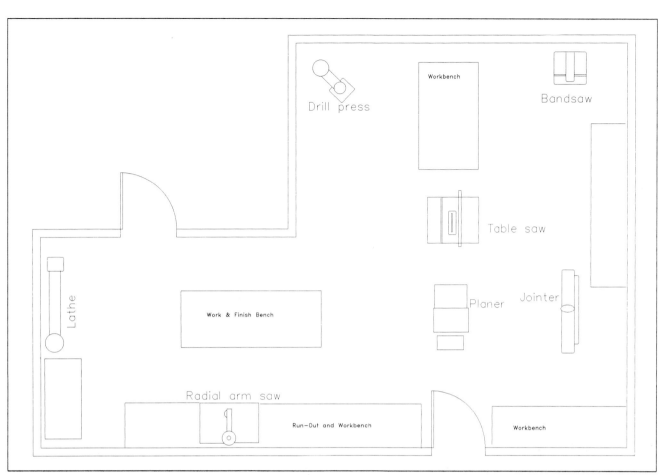

This is an "L" shop plan designed with *AutoSketch*.

This is a final floor plan for my upcoming shop.

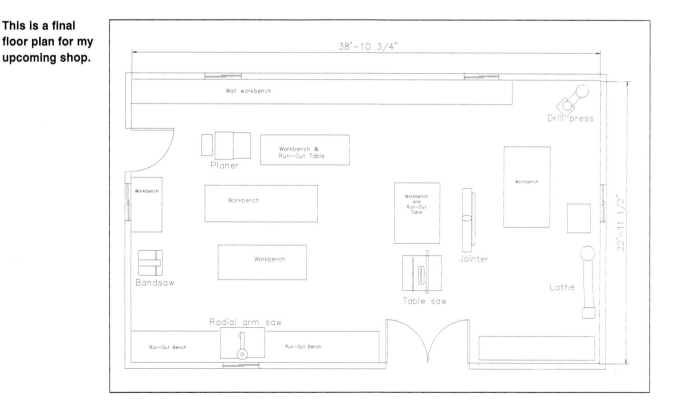

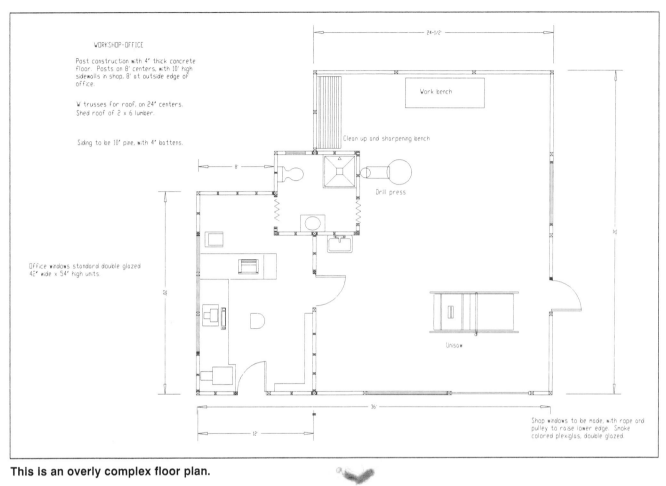

WORKSHOP-OFFICE

Post construction with 4" thick concrete floor. Posts on 8' centers, with 10' high sidewalls in shop, 8' at outside edge of office.

W trusses for roof, on 24" centers. Shed roof of 2 x 6 lumber.

Siding to be 10" pine, with 4" bottens.

Office windows standard double glazed 42" wide x 54" high units.

Work bench

Clean up and sharpening bench

Drill press

Unisaw

Shop windows to be made, with rope and pulley to raise lower edge. Smoke colored plexiglas, double glazed.

This is an overly complex floor plan.

This 6″ × 6″ pressure-treated post is buried 3′ deep. Is 3′ deep enough in your area? Check codes locally.

CHAPTER 2

ARRANGING WOODSHOP SPACE

———————■———————

There are both theoretical and practical layout considerations concerning space needs and general requirements for each tool. While table saws and radial arm saws do many of the same jobs, their uses and limitations make space requirements for the two quite different. This affects both tool placement and overall shop layout. The types of projects you want to build and the wood you wish to use and store will affect the layout of the shop. Those who never use plywood do not need the same space in layouts as those who do, and long board use requires appropriate storage space. It is possible to design a shop to handle both, but some compromises may be needed when space is tight.

At WoodenBoat the staff and students build wooden boats which take up a lot of space when being built.

PLYWOOD AND SHOP SIZE

Extensive use of plywood may require a shop larger than the size of one where most of the projects are constructed from boards. Today you'll find it difficult to locate solid wood that is more than a foot or so wide, which means you will have far different space requirements than if you use panels that are consistently

Having a large door in your shop can really help. No problem getting materials in, no problem getting projects out.

Here valuable tool storage space is wasted. Does your shop bench look like this?

4' wide and 8' long. You can buy plywood in other dimensions, but the 32-square-foot panel is by far the most common.

Plywood needs more storage space than boards. The most important need is the space to feed that large panel into your tools until it's cut down to manageable size. Usually plywood can be rough-cut with a cir-

cular saw a little wider than the size you actually need and then edge-trimmed to size on the table saw.

Once plywood is cut to size it requires no more space than regular boards, so spacing of tools is then similar. If plywood is the only material you will work with, your shop may well forego such tools as planers and jointers.

WOOD STORAGE

Wood can be stored outside your shop. Keeping 50 to 100 feet of board inside the shop would be nice, but it is usually impractical. Storing a large lumber supply indoors can create many problems. Even the massive cabinet and furniture shops don't store more than a few days' supply indoors. It uses up valuable heated space, which can be awfully expensive. If you plan to keep a lot of wood on hand, store only your more immediate needs in the shop. Construct a shed to keep the weather off other wood supplies. Instead of building a shed you can use a tarp, or section of metal roof, to cover the pile. Be sure to use a high-quality tarp to cover wood, not the lightweight woven poly tarps. The lower-quality tarps will often transfer color when whipped by the wind, and they do not stand weather well and will deteriorate to the point of leaking within a short period of time, even as little as three weeks.

Make sure any outdoor pile is stickered. This is the process of stacking lumber so that $3/4'' \times 3/4''$ "stickers" are spaced every 2' along the length of the boards to keep them from warping and, at the same time, allowing air to circulate around the entire board. And keep the first layer up off the ground at least 6".

USING SPACE REQUIREMENTS TO THEIR BEST ADVANTAGE

Space is always a workshop problem. There is seldom enough space for the tools you have, or would like to have. Several years ago, I rented an 18½' × 63' basement for use as a shop. My wife asked what I'd do with all that space. It took some weeks to clean up, paint floors and walls, and wire to accept modern loads from power tools; during that time, the empty expanse of floor looked imposing. By my sixth month in there, I was complaining of lack of space.

About the same time, a friend started constructing his freestanding workshop. He was moving from a 10' × 20' basement space into a 24' × 40' frame shop with wood heat. This man is one of the best I've ever seen at picking up old tools and getting them to work. He can find old cabinets and similar items to use in outfitting a shop. (He bought these old school cabinets at top right from me.)

As you can see, his is an overcrowded shop. Suffice to say, when a few boards are laid in, and one or two projects are partially finished — which is the normal state of affairs — the shop is hurting for space.

The moral: There ain't no such thing as enough space for any woodworker who ever gets serious. But we can and must try to increase efficiency, safety and pleasure in our hobby or small business.

Mobile Bases

To help you maximize space, HTC Products, based in Michigan, manufactures a wide line of mobile bases for woodworking machinery. The company provides wheeled bases for

An old shop class workbench and cabinet. Keeping an eye out for sales and auctions can really save you time and money.

Small planers can be easily moved when on sturdy stands.
Courtesy of HTC.

table saws, band saws, drill presses, jointers, planers and other tools. Such bases can make it practical to have tools pushed against the walls, rolling them out only when they're needed. (HTC Products, Inc., 120 E. Hudson, P.O. Box 839, Royal Oak, MI 48068. Phone (800)624-2027.)

I've used several of the bases and have been impressed with the quality, fit and ease of use.

TOOL SELECTION

Tool selection is integral to shop design and layout and requires as much thought as does shop layout in general. You place a 10″ or 12″ lightweight planer in a different manner than you do a 15″ or 20″ heavyweight planer. The same holds true for most stationary and benchtop tools. There's always a way to get a job done, no matter how large the job or how small the shop. You may have to move large plywood sheets outdoors to make preliminary cuts, or do your basic wood-planing outdoors, moving the project in as it reaches its smaller, more finished stage. You may find the selection of a lightweight table saw is an imperative. I have a lightweight table saw that can be used anywhere, and is easy to move around. Some table saws, like the *Delta Unisaw*, can weigh as much as 600 pounds – not an inducement to considerations of portability.

The objective is to create a workshop in which you can handle wood in ways unique to you, using tools and ideas based on those who have preceded you in the field. The first chapter showed how to plan the space to accommodate those tools that meet your needs. Here I want to

Tool stands for the shop.
Courtesy of HTC.

help you arrange the space those tools occupy in a manner that will best suit your needs.

Working from the main tool down, we'll start with saws and discuss their size and placement needs for different kinds of woodworking.

TABLE SAWS

The table saw is the basic stationary woodworking power tool in most shops, although some woodworkers, lathe workers for example, don't use one. Some general woodworkers use radial arm saws instead of table saws, and others prefer the bandsaw to all other saws. The standard full-size table saw will have a surface of about 24″ × 36″. Some table saws have much larger tables, up to 28″ × 40″ or more. You can always add to your table saw's surface area by making your own table extensions or purchasing them from the manufacturer.

Table Saw Spacing

Spacing around a table saw is critical to safe woodworking. Even as a benchtop tool, the table saw needs an acceptable run-in area with a run-

out area just as long. If you do a lot of sheet work, you'll find yourself needing greater width at the sides of the saw than otherwise. Remember, you can rough-cut sheet goods with a circular saw and finish dimensions off on the table saw. Long board crosscuts are generally more easily made with radial arm saws and power miter saws. You may also get a panel-cutting saw setup, but those are single-use tools and are quite costly.

Because the table saw is one of the primary tools, it is best located near an entrance or an exit so that wood may come directly to it. It is also a tool that works with a lot of long wood lengths, so needs a lot of space.

A good rule of thumb is to allow the size of the table saw plus 9′ in front of the saw for 8′ board ripping capability, with at least 8′ in back of the rear rip fence support for the long boards to move. That does not mean you actually need a space of 19½′ permanently clear in front and in back of each table saw. The saw may be backed up to a door in tight places, or face a door. You may use the back table for other things most of the time.

Your working habits can affect your space needs. Many people today work with precuts, i.e., wood lengths that are seldom as much as 4′ long and not often more than 6″ wide. Certainly, you don't need 9′ of run-in space with a 2′ or a 4′ board. But you do need enough clear foot space around the front and rear of the saw to make handling material safe. If a saw is set in an area full of extension cords, air hoses, board ends, or any other kind of clutter, you may bump such junk and end up with a finger or five in the blade. Anything that detracts from your paying complete attention to the work going on, and this is particularly true with the table saw, creates a safety hazard.

Minimum table saw space is about 6' wide by 8' deep, though not necessarily in a block that size. You must have room to handle the wood for rips, but those require only a pass up the center near the blade.

Safety

Recently I cut an 18″ square from plywood with no guards on the table saw. I moved a scrap of wood away with my left foot, when suddenly the 18″ square came back and whacked my chest with amazing force. Running the blade the standard ⅛″ above the wood, I'd allowed my push to relax a bit while concentrating on the scraps. The wood rode up over the blade, which immediately kicked it back, fortunately hitting me on a muscle that is fairly thick. It hit corner first, and I shudder to think what had happened if it had hit me in my neck, mouth, eye . . . use your imagination.

The cause had to be stupidity because it surely wasn't ignorance. I

knew better. Working without guards is just plain unsafe. And table saw kickback is rough. I've had small saws — 1 horsepower hobby models — ram chunks of oak back an inch or more deep into plaster walls.

So keep clutter down, and leave the guards on your saws!

Table Saw Sizes

My current bench saw system is small but very wide. With my miter kit and extension table kit both in place and extended, the saw can end up being almost 9' wide. Normally, it works at about 6' ½″ wide. The table offers advantages. It will also serve as a router table or jigsaw table.

A good space recommendation for a 10″ table saw with standard fence and table is 6' to the left of the saw, 4' to the right, 10' to the rear, and 10' to the front. Those figures are adjustable to suit. The spaces do not have to be totally open if you can clear them when necessary.

RADIAL ARM SAWS

Radial arm saws serve to do a few jobs that don't work well on table saws.

Some hobbyists use radial arm saws as base saws for an entire workshop and do very well with them. Most of us use them for special applications such as cut-offs, dentil work, and any form of top visible dado or molding work that is necessary. As I stated earlier, radial arm saws are not the tool of choice for rip sawing. They're basically unsafe even though they can do a good job.

Size

Radial arm saw sizes vary. Saw cost doesn't always make a difference in table size. Some tables tend to be a little larger than others, yet can be half the price. Still, radial arm saws aren't that hard to place. They're best set against a wall, with a dust collection system placed to draw from the back of the table. For best use in crosscutting and shaping long boards, the jobs at which the radial arm saw shines, 12' on each side of the table, and 3' in front of the saw, is a good recommendation. These recommendations hold for saws right up to 18″ diameter.

Placement

It will be rough to find a full 27' or so of unused wall space in any hobby shop and in most small commercial shops. Placing the radial arm saw near the center of a wall that is occupied mostly by workbenches should do it. In basement and other shops, the full length is not essential. Go with what you can usefully get, and

Special accessories such as the *HTC Brett Guard* and the roller outfeed table and mobile base make a large production saw easily movable. The unit is huge with all the additions, but it moves easily when necessary.
Courtesy of HTC.

make the saw mobile. With the aid of a couple of supports, you can then move the saw outdoors or into a roomier area to do your superlong cutting. Most cuts with the radial arm saw will be in much shorter stock, so that having 6' or even less on each side is perfectly acceptable in small shops. The 3' in front of the saw is essential for safe working. I'd also make sure the saw came out from the wall easily. Radial arm saws without dust collectors tend to build up a great deal of dust behind, and it is a good idea to make clean-up an easy job. Use a dust collection system whenever possible.

A radial arm saw with a custom enlarged table that backs against a wall and has its own dust collection system.

PLANERS

Planers are not shop essentials. However, in recent years, benchtop portable models have been introduced at affordable prices, allowing us to use our selections of rough lumber at lower cost.

Planers, like table saws, require a long run-in and run-out space depending on your desires for board length. For tight shop spaces, I'd suggest setting up a planer in front of a door, on a bench or stand that allows you to use the table saw table as a run-out area.

It is seldom these days that sawmills cut boards longer than 16'; most are in 10' or 12' lengths. You can handle much of the work from one side, since individual 1" × 6" or 1" × 8" boards aren't exceptionally heavy, even in white oak. Take strength into consideration, just as you do the normal sizes of wood with which you work.

Size

Planers vary in size. I own one that is a 12" model. That's close in size to most brands of portable 12" planers. The table extends out to only about 22" × 20" with steel legs, or a 23" × 22" rectangle with a shop-built stand. Lead-in space needs only to cover an 18" wide area. Look for lead-in and run-out spaces of whatever length you expect your boards to be, adding about 20" for the planer. For floor-mount planers in larger sizes the planer head might force you to add as much as 2' to the above figures, but most hobby shop planers will be 15" and smaller, with the planer head seldom more than 20" deep. Overall, you end up with a need for a space about 18" wide and 18' to 30' long. Most of us can't afford to keep that kind of space free for a single tool. The portable planer is affordable, being about half the cost of floor-mounted models.

Space Requirements

A good recommendation here is for 12' leading into the planer and 3' to the adjustment side of the planer. You need an equal distance to accept the boards coming out of the planer. That gives upward of 27'. Adjust yours according to your particular needs.

Collecting Dust and Shavings

Planers turn out an incredible pile of shavings with some rapidity, so have a dust system that can handle it. Remember to always wear a mask and be in a position to sweep the shavings aside until you have time to clean around the planer. The shavings can build up quickly, so you may want to take the time to stop and clean them up periodically to keep the area safe. One of the problems with a portable planer is its ease of movement. This makes it difficult to set up for long-term dust and chip removal. The chips and shavings are easily bagged. Cedar shavings repel fleas and are aromatic which helps to keep dogs comfortable.

JOINTERS

Jointers are essential tools in most power tool shops. You can make a jig

Portable planers let you buy and store rough lumber and plane it later.
Courtesy of Ryobi.

The lightweight jointer.
Courtesy of Delta.

that will get two edges of a board parallel for your table saw, but it won't give you the planed, finished edge the jointer will. And you'll usually find making chamfers, bevels and tapers far easier on a jointer than on a table saw.

The jointer is another tool that is prone to kicking back, and it is a tool where your fingers work exceptionally close to the turning blades. The guards must be in place and in good shape. Always work with sharp blades. This is one tool where I do *not* remove guards for better photography. If the camera can't get it, forget it.

Space Requirements

The space required is generally small; most jointers are less than 1' wide, with blade widths from 4" to 6", and less than 60" long. And most are light enough to be easily moved. You can lift or pull them into place for use when you need them. Like most power tools, jointers get more use when they occupy their own slots. A good space recommendation is 6' in front and 6' in back, plus 3' to one side of the jointer.

The space needs for width aren't great. You need the bare 12" width of even 6" blade width jointers, plus enough room for you to stand alongside the jointer and feed the material through. That will vary, of course. Overall, you shouldn't need more than 3' for the length of the jointer, plus the board width space over the blades, seldom more than 6".

For general use, a 40" jointer with 24" of space at each end is probably fine, which means less than 7½' of permanent space assigned. Jointers are easily wheeled around on mobile bases.

BAND SAWS

Band saws are exceptionally useful tools with many applications. They have the ability to cut curves, rip and crosscut stock, cut cabriole legs, and perform many other functions.

Band saw size varies. The most common band saw sizes for hobby shops are 12″ and 14″. This figure is the distance you can cut when going for the center of a board. Most band saws will fit in an 18″ × 18″ space. A mobile base increases that a bit. A good space recommendation is 4′ from the table on all sides of the saw.

Keep interference with your work lines to a minimum, as you must do with any woodworking tools, and you'll find that for most projects the band saw requires very little space.

DRILL PRESS

Drill presses for the small shop come in two versions, benchtop and floor-mounted. Space requirements aren't the same for both. I've got a couple of the benchtop models and find they take almost no space, less than 14″ square on any bench. Floor-mounted 15″ and larger drill presses can do just about anything any hobby woodworker is ever likely to want. This includes everything from drilling tiny, precise, ³⁄₆₄″ holes on up to drilling 3′ long ½″ holes in hardwood lamp bases. Even for such a large tool, the space requirement is minimal. A good recommendation is 3′ on each side of the drill press table, plus 3′ in front of the table. I wouldn't squeeze this, though a lot of people do stand the drill press at an angle in a corner. I like it at least 5½′ from the nearest obstruction on each side for those times you need to run holes near the ends of 6′ boards. Still, placing the unit on a wall so that it is

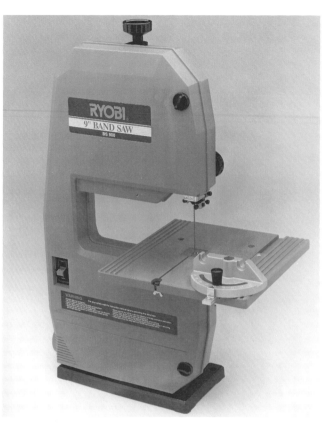

The benchtop band saw.
Courtesy of Ryobi.

advanced slightly over other tools of similar table height — remembering it is the table height that is adjusted on a floor drill press — seems to work well.

This is another tool that works well on wheels. You may want to make your own base because there is little or no thrust added to create problems with movement against the wheels.

SCROLL SAW

Scroll saws are delightful tools that provide a great deal of fun. They're also among the best tools for beginning woodworkers, because they're one of the safest and easiest to use. The scroll saw is far less likely to injure seriously than the table saw, radial arm saw, jointer and other power tools. That's not to say scroll saws can't hurt you. Always pay close at-

tention to that blade, or you are liable to get hurt. I've almost split the ends of fingers several times by not paying close attention.

Space requirements for scroll saws are small, and the portability of the tool is greatest among stationary saws. Even the heavy-duty industrial models lend themselves to being picked up and carted several feet by one strong person.

Space Requirements

Like all stationary tools, scroll saws present different size considerations. Many offer a 15″ cutting depth, but some go to 24″ and beyond. A good recommendation is to plan on at least 3′ on three sides. Most scroll saw work is small, so you need space to move the saw around to get the most effective angle for intricate cuts.

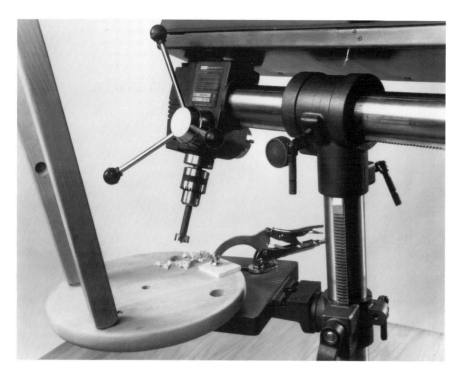

This radial drill press offers very easy angle drilling.

A low cost scroll saw. Great for beginners.

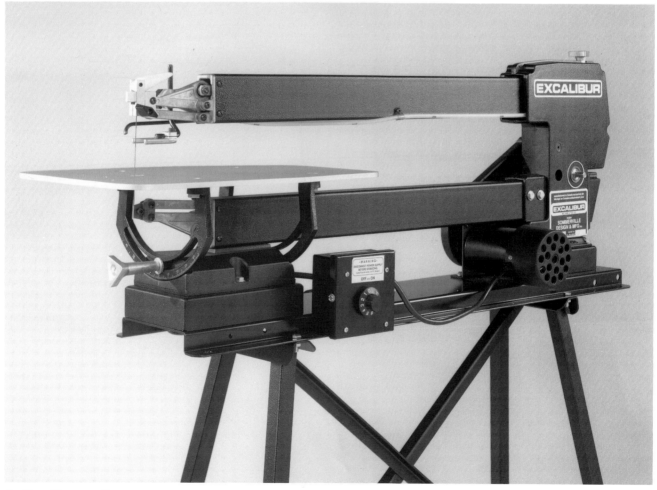

An Excalibur scroll saw.

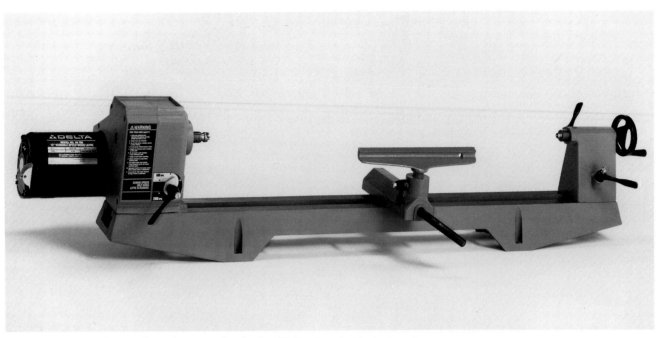

A wood lathe. It offers 12″ turning over the bed, with the head able to turn to allow 16″ bowl turning.

LATHE

Lathes are another tool that can be more or less backed against a wall and left in place, to be brought to a work area as needed. A good recommendation is 4′ to the left of the head stock and 3′ in front for the operator's stance along the entire length of the bed. Since most hobby lathes are not much longer than 3′ at the bed, and about 5′ to 6′ overall, you need a space of 9′ or 10′ along the wall. You also need some way to gather up shavings. Lathes require some light plywood or sheet metal work and some ingenuity to duct their wastes to a dust collecting system.

If you use a massive bowl lathe, you must do some figure conversion because the bowl lathes may have no actual bed and a truly massive throw to allow you to cut large diameter bowls. Most lathes have a throw of 12″ or less. With bowl lathes, you must move out from the wall to allow yourself access around large bowls. I suggest stationing such a lathe at least 4′ from any wall on the working end. You may want to butt the other end against a wall. You must use good judgement and the guidelines that I have outlined here to make your lathe space requirements fit your particular needs.

SHAPERS AND ROUTER TABLES

With the popularity of the router table, and the router arm, the shaper is becoming almost obsolete in today's small shop. Still, the space needs of both are similar. You need space behind and around the tool to make adjustments and bit changes. You need space in front of the tool for yourself. You need a long run-in and run-out space. I worked in a factory that manufactured church furniture, and we spent a great deal of time using a shaper for long runs. Pieces like pew backs, choir loft rails and similar items were done on the shaper. There wasn't anything unusual in running an 18' long piece of oak through the shaper to form a rail.

In general, it's not necessary to leave that much space behind and in front of a shaper or router table. Such occasions are infrequent, and the space can usually be cleared if it becomes necessary. A 6' space on all sides of the shaper is plenty to cover anything. You need the large operator movement area because both router tables and shapers are often used to shape pieces that extend toward the operator a considerable distance — items like door panel tops, sides and bottoms, for instance.

Overarm routers are available from numerous sources. Leave 6' on three sides of the tool, and you should be able to handle most situations.

Planer/molders aren't a new development in woodworking, but availability at lower cost is.

GRINDERS

Grinders may be mounted on benches or on pedestals. Size variations here are fairly small, but you need a few feet on each side of the grinder, plus 3' in front for the operator. A good recommendation is 3' from the wheels for each side of a 7" or 8" pedestal grinder, and 1' on each side for the 6" bench grinder.

Much depends on location. You should be able to work with 3' on each side. Many people use the flats of the wheels for some grinding.

SANDERS

There are many types of sanders, so space considerations will vary greatly. By mentioning a few here I hope to give you a sense of the space needed to plan for sanding. Most sanding is done on or around your workbench, so you will want to plan for portable sander storage near the bench. You will need a floor-mounted belt sander or sanding station close to your bench also. A sanding station consisting of a 6" × 48" belt sander with a 9", 10" or 12" disc will specify space. A good recommendation would be about 4' on each side. This unit can be put on wheels and stored against a wall until needed. You will find that you use this a lot, so try to plan a permanent space for it. My stationary belt sander has a 4" wide belt and a 6" disc, and I use it simply clamped onto a collapsible bench. Pieces being worked on these sanders are of moderate size, so you won't need long run-ins or long run-outs. Assembled or partly assembled boxes, birdhouses, cabinet frames, doors or panels typify the things most often worked on such units, though there are all kinds of uses for them.

Always try to allow sufficient space

Grinders are marvelous benchtop tools. They're great for sharpening and grinding.

Courtesy of Skil.

Benchtop belt-disc sanders don't have the capacities of full-sized models, but they clean and shape smaller profiles very effectively.

to be comfortable working at the machine. Some belt sanders are as much as 3' wide. These are often used to sand down counter tops and tabletops, making the length of the feed and run-out important. Most hobby shops will not have such sanders, but they're great labor-savers when available. You get a really good look at how perfectly flat a surface can be when you see what these can do for a counter top or benchtop.

AIR TOOLS

Air tools in the woodshop are becoming more and more popular, accessible and affordable for the home shop. Tools with air capabilities range from sanders to nailers to finishing equipment. I do very little high-pressure spray finishing, but I find the staplers, finish nailers and various sanders so handy I won't be without one.

If you have a compressor, you need to make room for it. Vertical tank models are probably the best buys for the woodworking shop, if the tool is to be stationary; if it isn't, the choices are extremely wide. Compressors can be in a confined area also. This is actually desirable because of the noise that a compressor can make. If you consider a stationary compressor, remember that there is no limit to the amount of hose you can run to use air tools. The compressor can be stored overhead, behind a wall or in a closet. Stationary setups usually start with a 60-gallon tank and a 5-horsepower compressor, but you can go larger. For a standard portable electric setup, almost any 3-horsepower, 20-gallon tank and up will do.

An angled head framing nailer for use with an air compressor. Buy or rent one to build a freestanding shop or to do any major construction work. Smaller and lighter units drive brads and finishing nails.

This air compressor is not much more costly than some wheel-mounted models but offers 5 horsepower and a 60-gallon vertical tank, instead of the more common 3 or 3.5 horsepower from horizontal portable models. The vertical model also takes up just about half the floor space of a horizontal model.

BENCHES

Benches vary from design to design, and this is really something you must choose on your own. I will give a few examples here, but you can find myriad styles and setups to suit your particular needs. I will not even begin to look over the types of benches available that you can buy preassembled or build. I figure I've used at least one hundred types of benches over the years.

At this moment, I have three collapsible benches and two 8′ long benches of my own construction, and I expect to build at least four more benches. Remember, used kitchen or other cabinets make great frames for workbenches.

Bench Placement

Placement of benches depends on your work habits. I like at least one bench placed in the center of the floor, so that all four sides are accessible. That means with a 24″ wide bench a space of at least 8′ wide by 14′ long should do. A second bench against the wall is a good idea, about 22″ deep. Collapsible benches can go anywhere and store in a small space. They can even be hung up if possible. I have a friend who came across a bunch of school lab cabinetry rejects and placed them around three walls of his shop, giving him a huge amount of flat space. There's still not enough horizontal space, but that's the case in any workshop.

Try to always leave yourself 3′ of working space around sides of any bench that are intended to be accessible. You can often get away with 30″, but more is better in this case.

Bench construction is a personal thing, when it comes to the large central styles. Here are some plans for a

Another example of a collapsible bench.

The American Plywood Association Hobby Table requires only a half sheet (4' × 4') of ¾" plywood, plus a few other bits and pieces.

more mobile style that can be very useful in a small shop.

Hobby Table/Desk

This is a bolt-and-slot work table that only takes a few minutes to come out of a closet yet offers stable working space. You can make it from half a sheet of A-B, A-C or overlaid plywood. The final work area is 24" × 40", and the height is adjustable from 25" to 29". Designed for seated work, this table is also sturdy because of its wide legs and center brace.

These tool stands also serve as small benches when no tools are mounted.
Courtesy of HTC.

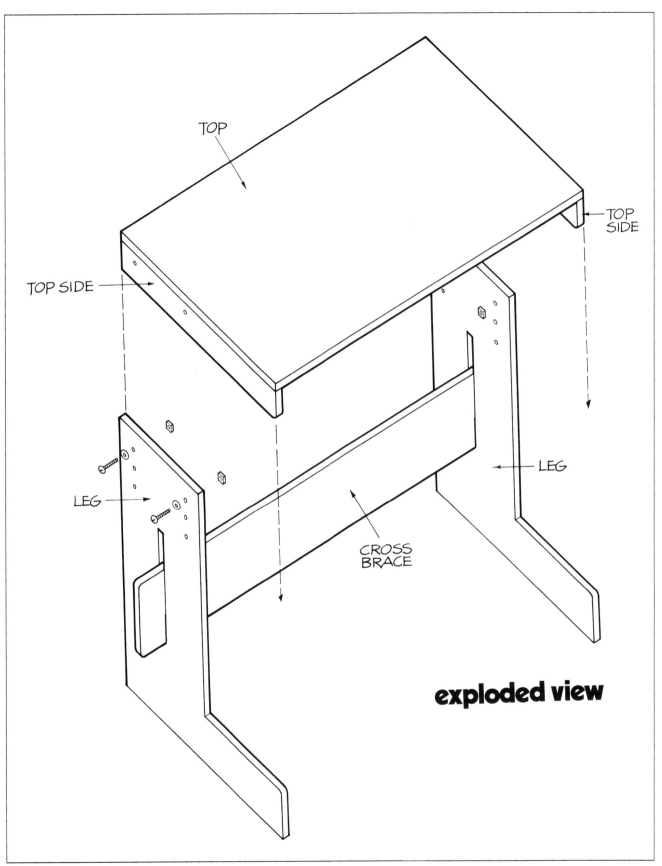

TOP

TOP SIDE

TOP SIDE

LEG

LEG

CROSS BRACE

exploded view

American Plywood Association plans and layout diagram.

Materials	**Tools**
½ sheet ¾" 4' × 4' plywood or MDO (medium density overlay)	Table or circular saw for straight cuts
	Jig saw or bayonet saw for curved or slotted cuts
4 ¼" × 2" stove bolts, with washers and nuts	Cordless drill
¼ pound 6d finishing nails	¼" drill bit
Yellow wood glue	Hammer
Wood filler	Nail set
150-grit sandpaper	Measuring tape
Tung oil or other fine-grade finish—stain is optional, or you may prefer to use paint, especially if you use MDO	Try square or combination square
	Scribe or pencil
	Random orbit or finishing sander

Begin by following the panel layout as shown on the drawings. Make sure you leave the required ⅛" for the saw kerfs along every line that separates parts. Where the ⅛" doesn't seem available, as with the leg brace, take it off the part that doesn't matter— in this case, the leg brace. You want all the top that you can get.

Lay the parts out and use 100-grit or finer sandpaper to clean up any splinters or chips on edges.

Assemble the top, with its two braces placed as shown, and glued and nailed together. Start nails until they're almost through the top. Run a bead of adhesive along the top of the top side pieces (do this one piece at a time, carefully, and finish the first side before gluing any of the second side. Most aliphatic resin adhesives take a set in about ten minutes, and you may need all that time to line up and nail one side.)

Drill the holes for the stove bolts after you've set the top in place on the braced legs. Make sure you back the holes to prevent splintering (place a piece of ¼" junk wood behind the holes). Fill all exposed edges with wood filler, and sand carefully. Sand overall, and either paint or stain and finish.

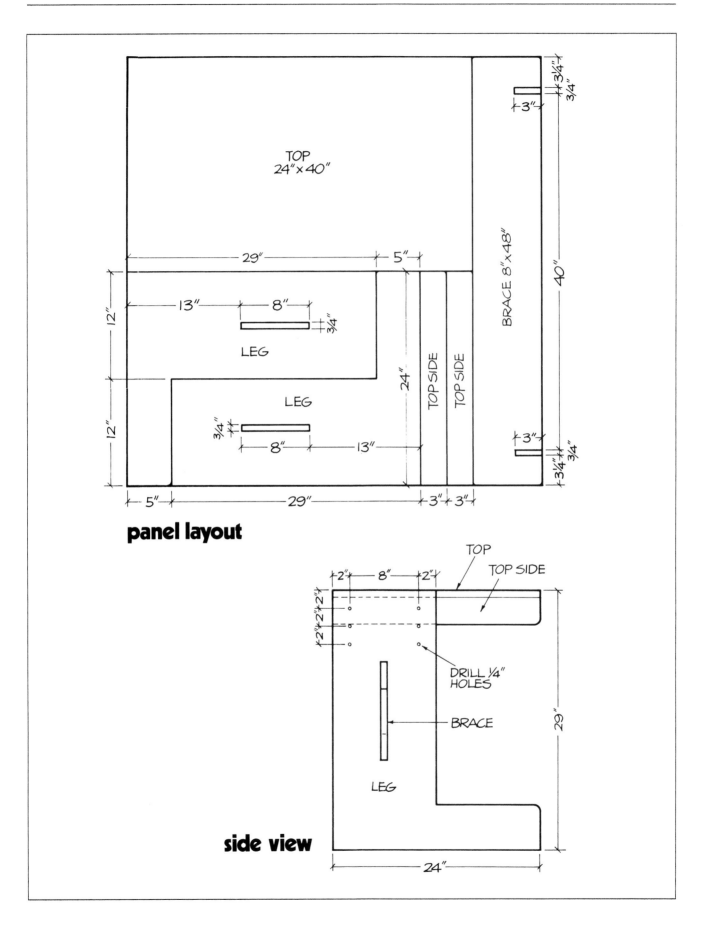

panel layout

TOP
24"×40"

BRACE 8"×48"

LEG

LEG

TOP SIDE

TOP SIDE

side view

TOP

TOP SIDE

DRILL ¼"
HOLES

BRACE

LEG

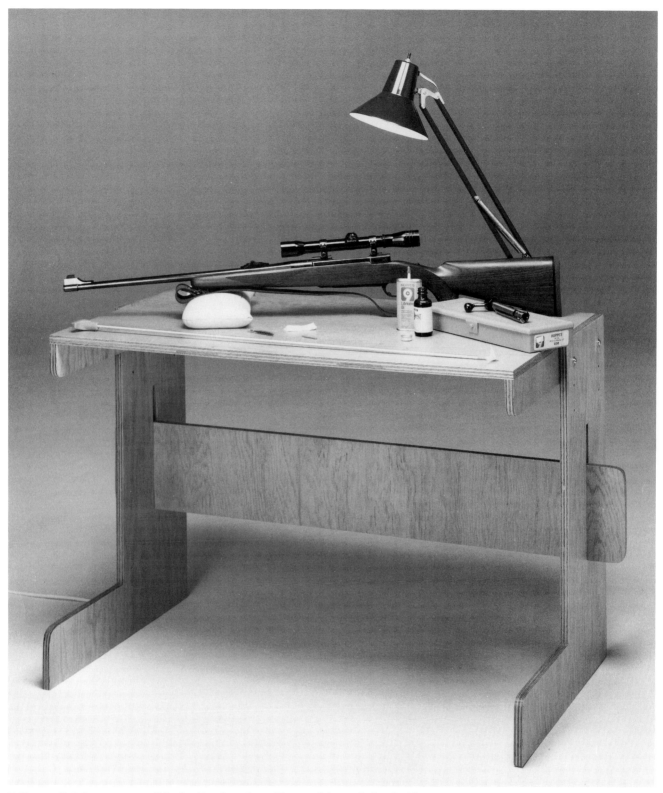

Different finishes are possible for the American Plywood Association hobby table.

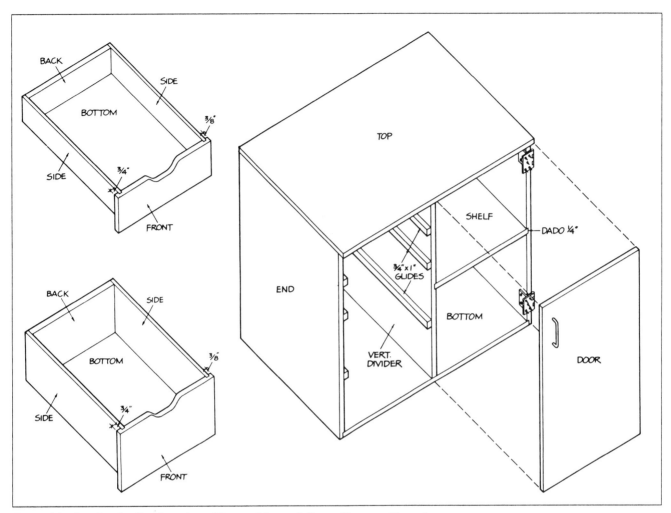

Assembly drawing for the American Plywood Association rolling workbench.

Rolling Workbench/ Storage Cabinet

For small and large workshops alike, there's never really enough worktop space. Woodworkers always complain about a lack of space. This project not only provides a reasonable amount of extra flat space, it is also portable and may be rolled right to the job. While the 2′ × 3′ top isn't the largest work surface, it is sufficient for projects up to medium size. The relatively small overall size makes this storage and work unit nearly ideal for apartments and smaller basement workshops.

Get a fast start here by marking the panels as the drawings show, allow-

ing ⅛″ for each kerf (saw cut slot). To ease the work, cut the full panels down to workable size: Cut the ¾″ panel lengthwise, 22½″ wide on one part. Cut the ½″ panel widthwise, 44½″ on one side (or make sure one side is at least 51½″). This makes the panels easier to deal with. Even the half panel can be cut so one side is 15½″ wide (the drawer backs come from this strip), easing overall handling.

Next, cut all pieces to final size, being careful to get the cuts to the accurate size.

Mark and make a ¾″ × ¼″ dado on the inside of one side, and run the ¾″ deep by ¼″ wide rabbet on the

---

Materials

1	¾″ × 4′ × 8′ A-B plywood
1	¾″ × 4′ × 4′ A-B plywood
1	½″ × 4′ × 8′ A-B plywood
2	fixed 2½″ locking casters
2	swivel 2½″ locking casters
16′	¼″ × ¾″ screen molding
1	pair 2½″ × ¾″ offset hinges
1	magnetic cabinet catch
4	drawer pulls (optional)
1	cabinet door handle
18	¼″ × #6 screws for drawer glides
48	1½″ × #6 screws for cabinet assembly

½-pound 4d finishing nails
½-pound 6d finishing nails
Wood glue
100- or 150-grit sandpaper
Paint, or stain and clear finish, as desired
Wood putty

Tools

Table or circular saw
Jig or scroll saw
Router
Edge guide
¾″ straight bit
¼″ rabbeting bit
½″ straight bit
Nail set
Cordless drill
³⁄₃₂″ bit for pilot holes and holes for handles
Screwdriver for hinge screws
Claw hammer
Measuring tape
Square
Finish sander or random orbit sander

---

bottom of both sides. The center divider gets a dado matching in distance down from the top the one on the inside of the right side. Install drawer glides in the positions shown, using glue and three 1¼″ nails, from the glide positions into the sides, for each glide. These go on the left side of the vertical divider and on the inside of the left end.

Set the bottom inside its rabbets on the bottoms of the sides, with glue, and drive 1½″ or 1⅝″ screws, four per end. Make sure the unit is square, and add the top, with ¼″ overhang at each end, using 6d nails and glue, nails spaced 3″ apart. Again, check to make sure it is square. Allow the glue to set for a couple of hours, longer if possible.

Insert the center divider into the marked places, and fasten with glue and screws.

Assemble the drawers, after cutting the handling arches and the ¼″ × ½″ dadoes. Use 4d nails and glue for assembly. Keep a check on square, even though the assemblies are small.

Install hinges on the door, and the door on the cabinet. Install the door handle and magnetic catch. Turn the unit upside down and install the casters with ¾″ screws. You may wish to screw and glue a ¾″ × 4″ × 4″ block inset ½″ in from each corner to allow the use of 1¼″ wood screws with the casters. Otherwise, use the ¾″ screws and inset ½″ from each side and end.

Remove the door hardware and the door. Sand the entire project with 100-grit sandpaper, and paint. Or sand with 150-grit sandpaper, and stain and coat to suit. Use only a light coat or two of low-gloss finish on the top. Left plain, the top can be recovered as needed after it gets battered by various kinds of work. To recover, use ¼″ plywood, or tempered hardboard, placed with contact cement.

Reinstall the door, and go to work.

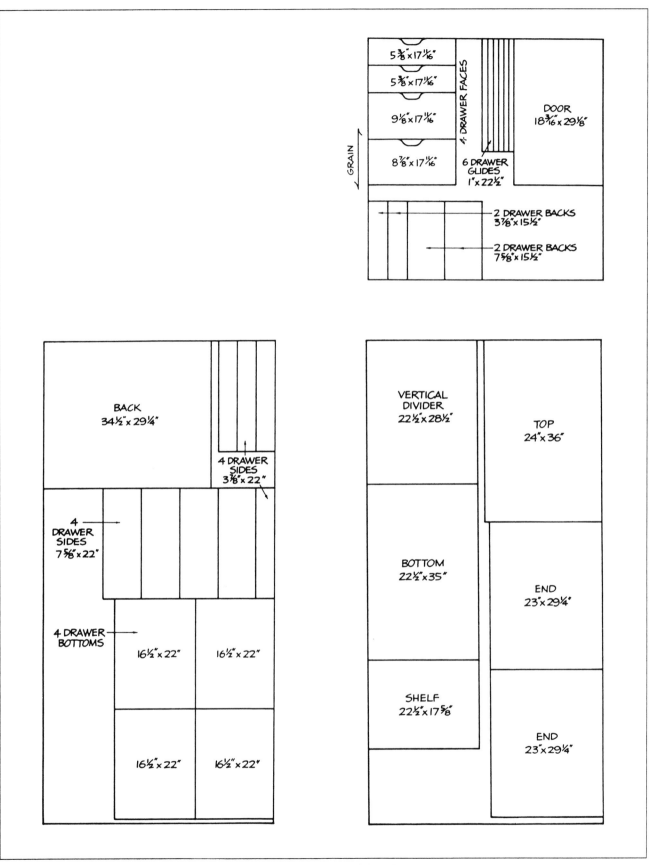

Layout patterns for the American Plywood Association rolling workbench.

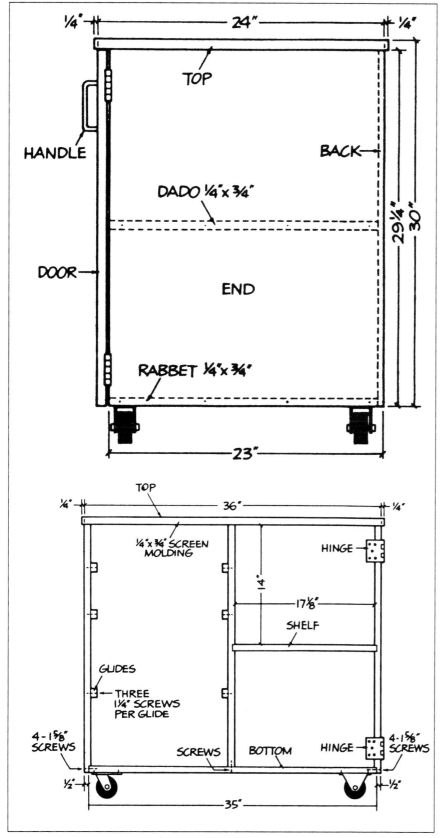

Front and side views of the American Plywood Association rolling workbench.

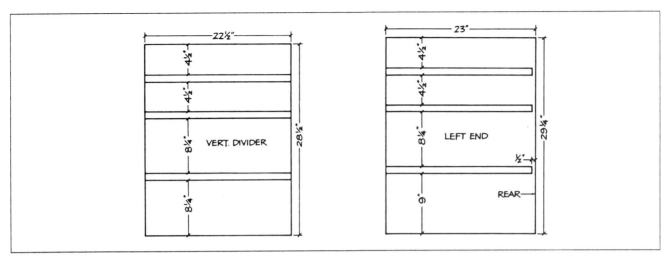

Drawer glide positions for the American Plywood Association rolling workbench.

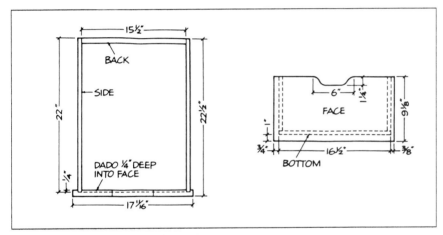

The 9⅛″ drawer for the workbench.

CHAPTER 3

HARMONIZING YOUR TOOL AND WORK NEEDS

T he most pleasing and enjoyable woodworking comes when you harmonize your shop design with the requirements of different tools and the space available.

TABLE SAW

As I said previously, the table saw is the basic power saw of use in almost all shops. The variations available today are far greater than ever before. Manufacturers have combined technology with new materials and designs to make table saws much more efficient, easier to use and safer than in the past. The possibilities range from a 10″ benchtop table saw that weighs less than 50 pounds to huge 12″ blade models that weigh well more than ten times that amount. There's a table saw for almost everyone who needs one.

In my opinion, you need a saw that will work to within 1/64″ for greatest accuracy—not to within microns

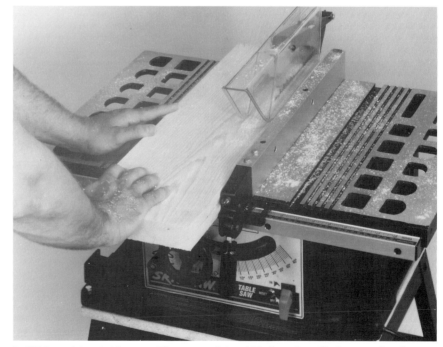

A 10″ benchtop table saw. These work best if placed on their own stand.

or thousandths of an inch. The saw must be able to maintain this tolerance consistently over time. I suggest that you make the investment to get a table saw that is made to maintain these close tolerances. With table

saws, as with a lot of other things, you get what you pay for.

Benchtop Models

The basic benchtop saw has improved greatly in recent years. These saws present a good solution for the basic woodworking shop, and the price is right. Most are available for around $200, and that figure is likely to drop as time goes on. Make sure you purchase one with a 10″ blade. You don't want a smaller blade size than this. Saws with a blade smaller than 10″ are not particularly well suited to larger shop-built accessories such as sliding miter tables. But they'll sure fill the bill for most small shops. I like to have one or more of these saws on hand for times when the standard shop saw is locked up on other jobs. And it's handy to have a relatively low-cost tool set to one side of the shop with a dado head in place, so you can make specialty cuts without breaking down the setup on the big saw. At today's prices, the serious woodworking hobbyist might well think about having two of these saws ready, one set for dadoing and one for use of a molding head.

The table saw's true place in the scheme of things is the rip cut—just the opposite of the radial arm saw, which does far better with crosscuts. Thus, you need extra devices to increase accuracy, and capacity, of mitering and crosscutting. The sliding table is the best of those devices.

Also available are wide table fence additions, a miter hold-down clamp, a dust bag, a stand, wheels and a dado insert.

Now we come to my basic complaint about lighter-weight table saws. The table inserts all require several operations for change. In most cases you must back out and remove one or two screws. Any table saw that has small parts like fasteners not easily replaced from shop stock are a nuisance and unsafe, because your work can get caught up in them. You

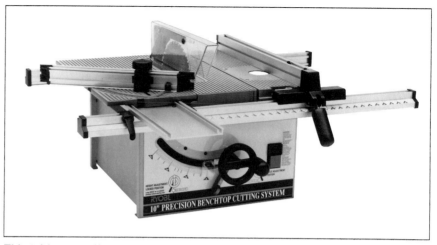

This table saw offers a sliding table. It is a new design and has many new features.

can make your own inserts for most saws out of ⅛″ stock.

You can also purchase light production models, a step up from the bench model table saw. These are on their own stands and are usually equipped with stronger motors, larger work surfaces and more sturdy construction. On some the miter gauge is a T-slot, with the horizontal slot on the bottom, so the miter gauge is held more accurately. Some models have a magnetic motor starter available, and I recommend it, as it keeps the motor from restarting if power is cut off from any place other than the switch.

RADIAL ARM SAWS
The basic advantage of the radial arm saw comes in crosscutting. It will rip, but is not as safe or accurate in rip work as the table saw.

Today's radial arm saws also accept router bits on an accessory shaft and they do all sorts of dadoing. The difference in using a radial arm saw to do dadoing is that you can actually see the cut, as opposed to the table saw, where you cannot. The radial arm saw is also great for squaring up

the ends of long stock, and when making miter, bevel and compound crosscuts in long stock. The radial arm saw has no limits on the length of the material it can cut.

Radial arm saws can be difficult to tune and keep in tune, so keep that in mind when selecting the basic saw

Radial arm saws do some jobs better than table saws, like molding head work and dentil trim.

for a shop. I would not use a radial arm saw as a basic saw. It is a superb supplementary tool that can do a great many things more easily than can a table or band saw, but it is not a replacement for a table saw and most certainly will not replace a band saw. With some quick adjustments and a few accessories, you can make the table saw a superb cut-off machine as well, but it will never be as good as the radial arm saw at crosscutting or making miter cuts.

Benchtop Models

Benchtop radial arm saws are available for the home shop. They are relatively small in capacity—the blade is only 8¼″ in diameter. A more desirable size is 10″: The 8¼″ size loses nearly an inch off cut depth compared to the 10″. The motor speeds in these saws tend to be high, which creates some problem with the blade climbing through work as it is fed. You must be conscious of the possibility and hold the power head back

to the proper feed, or the blade climbs and the motor stalls.

These saws offer an 18,500-speed accessory spindle on the side of the motor opposite the arbor for use with router bits. The high speed is good here, because router bits are designed to work at speeds over 10,000 rpm, and up to about 25,000 rpm.

I appreciate the radial arm saw for two things: You can get extreme depth in dadoes and, using a dado head or a molding head, you can get some fine multiple cuts and shapes because you are able to view the cuts. And it is fairly easy to set up to make multiple dadoes as you do when creating dentil moulding.

BAND SAWS

The band saw is a diverse tool and usually one of the most useful saws in the shop. You cannot cut, no matter how slowly, 6″ thick wood on your table saw or radial arm in a single pass, but you can on most 14″ and 12″ band saws. You cannot cut

curves on table and radial arm saws, but you can with the band saw.

The band saw lends itself to production cutting of complex parts in a process known as *layered cutting*. For example, if you had a pattern on a ¾″ stock that you need a lot of, you can tape pieces of the ¾″ stock together and cut them all at once.

Most band saws have available accessories to make ripping and cutting circles easy; the band saw is just about the only tool of choice when cutting round tabletops of any size. Blades are available that make scroll-cutting easier, as are blades that make ripping operations easier. Resawing with a band saw is tricky, even when using a fence, because the blade tends to follow the grain of the wood. New blades especially for this problem prevent the blade from straying.

Band saws are versatile tools that should be in your shop design. Sooner or later we all need to cut a curve, and it is often where a jigsaw will not work.

Band saws are the closest saw to being good enough at enough things to allow setting up a one-saw shop. Benchtop band saws are great for lighter work.

Courtesy of Sears, Roebuck & Co.

SCROLL SAWS

For intricate work there's nothing at all like a scroll saw. The blade moves up and down from a device that provides power in a spinning, circular motion. The connecting device is nothing more than a cam with an eccentrically mounted spindle shaft that provides an up-and-down action, in the same manner that a camshaft in an auto engine moves the valve shafts up and down. A blade-holding clamp moves with the same action. These are fixed-arm scroll saws with power provided through the upper arm to drive the blade downward, after which a compressed spring returns it to its position. Constant-tension saws use a rocker action on a C- or U-shaped frame, with the tension on the blade more nearly constant than with the cam spindle type. Another type offers parallel arms that rock in unison but are not a single unit.

The constant-tension models are considered more modern, but there are still some cam-spindle, fixed-arm types available.

Scroll saws do the intricate fretwork that has become so popular in recent years. They also do pierced cutting. Simply drill a hole in the work, remove the blade and thread it through the hole, and reinstall the blade. It takes only about a minute, maybe two on harder-to-work saws. The only other common stationary tool that does the same job is the band saw, and it requires a blade breaker and a blade welder to work. And you'd better hope you don't twist the break or overheat the weld!

A scroll saw is superb for anyone teaching youngsters the craft of power woodworking because it offers a modest powered tool with no kick-back problems. You can't say that about a table saw, shaper, radial arm saw, jointer or similar power tools.

If you build toys or like to cut intricate patterns in projects, a scroll saw is almost inevitable. Prices range from about $100 to thousands of dollars, depending on your needs.

JOINTERS

Jointers are necessary for most woodworking shops. You must be able to square up and smooth up two sides of a piece of wood before you can carry out further operations with any accuracy. Buying all wood cut to size for each project would be very expensive. A jointer will save you money and time in the long run. Jointers come in a wide array of types, sizes, power requirements, capabilities and price.

The light-duty models offer a 4″ blade width, a table less than 2′ long, and a modestly powered motor. A step up from those is 6″ jointers. Some manufacturers offer new capabilities, like the jointer-planer. The table is short for a 6⅛″ jointer, possibly the shortest of all, but there's an accessory set of extensions that work nicely to expand stability. The unit does not offer a rabbeting ledge, which is something of a major lacking in some shops. Overall weight is about 27 pounds, and even with a steel stand it is well under 50 pounds, so it does not require much in the way of dedicated floor space.

There are also larger types such as the 8″ up to 16½″ to 17″. Unless you've got exceptional needs, any of the 6″ jointers will do you well. Benchtop planers can solve small problems like squaring-up difficulties in the small shop or in shops where wood use is minimal, such as shops that do framing or make small boxes. You will need a jointer, but 4″ should do it.

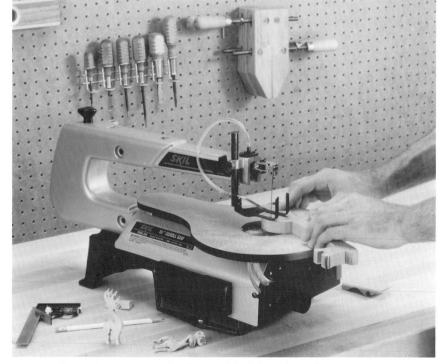

The scroll saw is a great tool to learn with. It is safe and easy to use.

Jointers are essential for moderate to advanced woodworking.

Courtesy of Ryobi America.

PLANERS

The invention of the portable planer started many woodworkers on the road to lower-cost woodworking. The planer can reduce wood cost in

Planers can reduce wood costs considerably.

Courtesy of Sears, Roebuck & Co.

any shop and can make it far simpler to get the exact thickness of wood you need without forcing you to depend on local sources for planing. You can buy locally available hardwoods and allow them to air dry, planing them after a year or so and reducing your cost considerably. For a few cents per board foot, you may be able to locate a place in your area that will finish dry your stock in a kiln. Add that to custom planing and careful jointing, and you can do more work at lower cost.

Portable and Stationary Planers

Most 10″ and 12″ portable planers are considerably cheaper than are 12″ stationary planers. Portable benchtop models are high-speed machines that give a more polished finish to the wood. They also have a tendency to snipe the ends of the wood as it comes out of the planer. *Snipe* is a cupped cut at or near the end of a board, and the only real defense with these planers is to make sure the board has an additional foot overall

so you can cut off the snipe and use it for kindling in your wood stove.

SANDERS

A wide variety of stationary power sanders is available for small shops. There are 1″ belt sanders, 4″ belt sanders, 6″ belt sanders, disc sanders from 4″ to 12″, flap sanders, drum sanders to 36″ wide, short- and long-edge sanders and many others. Unless you plan to do huge amounts of counter top or similar building, the wide-drum sanders aren't necessary—and they're not cheap. The same holds true for edge sanders, and flap sanders are only a help when you do much sanding of uneven surfaces. For normal amounts of such sanding, you are better off with a 4″ belt sander and a disc sander setup.

MULTIPURPOSE TOOLS

The multipurpose tool is a different thing in European concept than it is in North America. Some European models stay on the market here fairly consistently. The best example of the multipurpose tool is the *Shopsmith*. The *Shopsmith* line of multipurpose tools is a series of moderate-cost hobby tools for use in shops where space is limited. The basic tool includes a table saw, lathe, drill press, horizontal boring machine and disc sander.

Additions are available that can be powered and mounted on the base unit or separately. You may add a 6″ × 12″ belt sander, a band saw, scroll saw, planer, jointer, moulding heads and others.

With the multipurpose tool you get a good, useful array of tools. Further on the pro side, the entire unit is on wheels and is easily stored at the end or side of a garage that must house a vehicle or two. And it slips under basement stairs pretty easily.

HANDWORK OPTIONS

Equipping a shop means a lot more than making a selection from the preceding tools. There are many hand tools with different woodworking aims. If you prefer handwork, you need to aim at a layout that includes more free benchtop space, plus a good bit of extra vise space. You may be more interested in a European-style workbench as a main bench, with its multiple array of excellent clamping devices, bench dogs, and other top-of-the-bench accessories.

WORKSHOP SPACE REQUIREMENTS AND TOOL PLACEMENT

You need to combine tool spaces to see what can and cannot be overlapped safely in the selection of tools needed to carry out your basic woodworking desires. Let's look at the table saw and the planer, for instance. Overlap the feeds for the table saw and the planer in one direction, and all may work well. But do it in the other direction, and problems crop up. For example, it may work well to have the planer feed into the front of the table saw after at least 8′ of runout space, but it is probably best not to have it run into the rear of the saw. It can overlap its feed with the table saw from the sides, of course, needing only for the blade to be retracted and the rip fence to be removed to make the saw a handy helper.

Planers and table saws do best when placed near the main entry door or doors, because they are the machines you're most likely to feed long stock into with frequency. Make it easy to get the stock to the tool,

Benchtop planers are lower in cost than planer/molder models and are exceptionally useful around the woodworking shop.

and you save time and energy. Taking your time and being well rested are both foundation stones of workshop safety.

Placing a planer so that its outfeed table runs the finished stock over a table saw depends on two things. First, the tables must be close to the same height, with the table saw lower than the planer. Second, you must set up so the chips and dust from the planer do not foul the table saw. The planer turns out more waste in the form of chips and dust than does any other tool.

Using planned infeed and outfeed overlaps, you can design a shop with many tools, yet relatively small space needs. I have a friend whose shop, though large for a hobby shop, has a lot of tools, including three table saws. Most of the tools are placed so

as to allow outfeeds over unused workbenches or over other tools.

He also uses portable benchtop tools with their ability to be stored out of the way in small areas. All his table saws feed onto workbenches built at exactly the same height as the saw tables, which are placed on stands he designed and built.

Planning to Save Space

No matter what size shop you create, there will be a need for some space saving. Even if you could afford to construct an aircraft hangar, you'd eventually fill it. Check the sizes of all your tools and of those you plan to buy. Draw a diagram on ¼″ graph paper close to scale, and make cardboard cutouts of the various tools and their placements. It's probably best, on major stationary tools such as the planer, table saw, jointer and band saw, that you make the cutouts of a size to include the infeed and outfeed needs of the tool. And mark the height of the tool's table, if known.

Most band saws have considerably higher tables than do table saws, scroll saws, sanders and so on, so they are readily and easily placed close to benches. Lathes are easy to place and require little room, but that room cannot safely be impinged upon. You need that 3' or 4' to the left of the headstock side of the lathe to make adjustments, and you must have the 3' along the full length of the lathe to work the materials without worrying about bumping into things.

Safe Work Habits

Leave yourself enough free space to concentrate on doing your work safely, regardless of which tool you're placing. It pays off in better and safer work. Don't waste space. Too much space between tools can be almost as bad as too little. You can run yourself ragged getting wood from one station to another.

Try to envision your working habits, based on the projects you build or intend to build. If you start with raw wood, you want a protected area to store the drying wood and a better-protected area to store wood that's finished drying. You want easy transfer from the first to the second, or to a vehicle if it is to be taken and kiln dried after air drying. The seasoned wood stack needs to be close by the door that leads directly to your planer. From there, you'll probably want to go to a radial arm saw or a power miter saw to cut the wood to length. After that you need a jointer

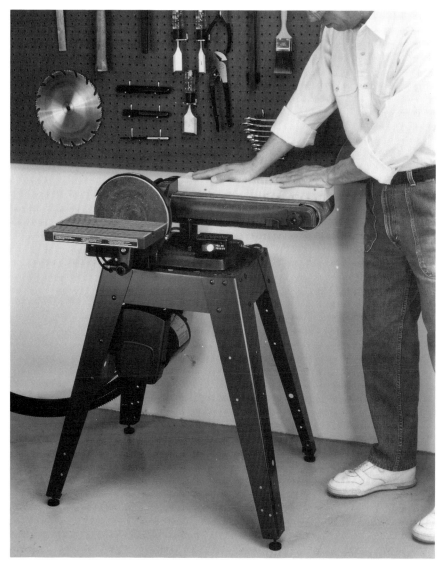

A 6″ × 48″ belt sander with 9″ disc.

The router table quickly becomes an essential tool as it expands the uses of almost any router.

Courtesy of Sears, Roebuck & Co.

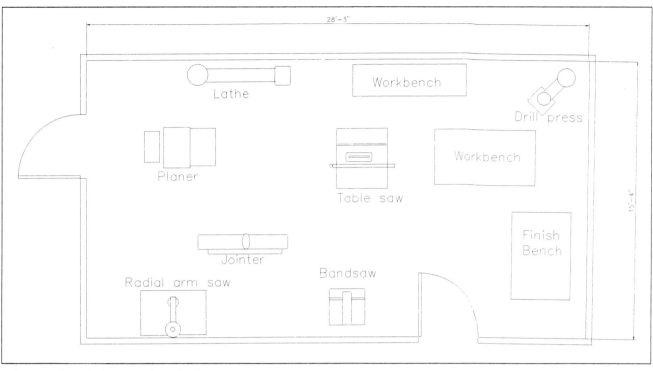

A fully equipped shop need not be huge.

and a table saw. Beyond the table saw you want your drill press and band saw. If you do a lot of lathe work, you will want it near the table saw, beyond a gluing bench where you might glue up sections for turning.

FINISH AREA

Store your finish under a bench, and keep the brushes covered under the same bench. Everything is brushed or blown clean before finishing is started, and the entire shop has to cease work on other projects when one is drying.

While spraying finishes give the smoothest and best coverage, they aren't suitable for all projects. Investing in air-compressing gear and spray guns becomes expensive. A good air compressor, tank and spray equipment cost several hundred dollars and take up some shop space.

I find sprayers invaluable, but I know many others who don't use

them at all. Your finish area may need some enclosure to protect it from dust and to protect other areas from overspray and fumes. If you enclose your area, use a spark-free fan to exhaust air to the outside.

In most small shops, spraying is moderate and special venting may not be needed. Good shop ventilation requires that you install windows to give good cross-ventilation.

You can also construct a small benchtop spray booth to house small projects while finishing and to reduce overspray and fumes while keeping airborne dust off drying projects. You can make these booths out of ¼″ plywood and a light frame, or of ½″ or thicker plywood and no frame. Make a 3′ to 4′ long box 2′ to 3′ high, depending on your needs, and 18″ deep. You may slant the top and sides so as to have better access around a piece. It works nicely with a cup hook or two placed in the top of the

booth, letting you hang small pieces and spray all sides in one operation.

GATHERING MATERIALS

Collecting materials to build a shop can save many thousands of dollars. It takes work and planning. You may want to attend auctions, sales, and the side rooms of housing product manufacturers to save money.

In my planning for shop construction, I've been able to save a great deal of money simply by listening to a friend or two and allowing one of my good friends to go ahead and buy things for me when I'm not around.

Don't get fixated on having all new equipment. I've got two interior doors, sitting and waiting for use, for which almost no money changed hands. They were the result of a change in plans for an industrial building, so they are good, fire-resistant, oak-faced doors that probably retail for more than $100 each.

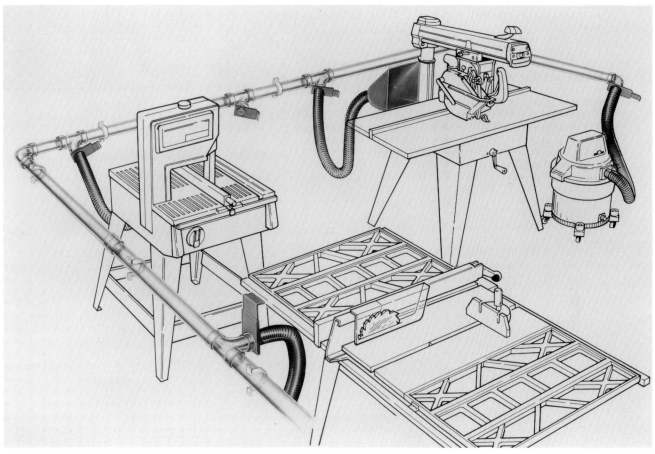

Many companies offer dust collection bits and pieces. This setup uses a single shop vacuum as its base unit and power source.

Locating cheap windows may present some problems, but most areas of the country have reinstallers (companies that replace old windows). Some do a neat job of removing old windows and are willing to part with those for very little money. Some will let you have them for the hauling. The same may hold true for doors.

As far as doors in the design go, you want the largest doors possible, without losing too much wall space. If you plan to build a boat or a similar project, see about doing the large assembly outdoors. That saves shop space and allows you to build a project of a large size without increases in shop size.

Check the "Items for Sale" col-umns in any local newspapers. There are usually several such lists, some of which even cover contractors' left-overs.

Drive around and check new home construction. Talk to supervisors on job sites and see if they're holding on to any extras that the supplier won't accept as returns. Most contractors today work out a return policy with suppliers, and most materials are returned, but there are exceptions. It is possible to save a considerable amount of money on insulating sheathing board, shingles and similar products.

Check yard sales, too. Some are worth fooling with, most aren't, but considering some of the things I've sold out of my front yard and bought out of others', it's worthwhile to make a quick stop at the larger sales. Feel free to haggle. Often, especially in rural areas, there's an outbuilding crammed with goodies that are too heavy — like floor joists or doors or windows — to tote out to the yard every time a sale is held.

Check for local manufacturers of building products. There is a large window and door manufacturer barely 45 miles away from where I live. It has overruns and returns of special orders, and non-pick-ups of special orders and similar stock at all times. And the prices are substantially reduced over similar-quality products at a dealer. I also have in my area a huge number of small sawmills producing all kinds of rough

The ToolMate is meant to hook up to individual tools.

Courtesy of ShopVac.

lumber from poplar and yellow pine. The number of mills helps keep prices down and also makes for fast delivery.

Look around for school sales and municipal building sales. As much as I hate to say it, a great deal of tax money is lost in early recycling of materials such as lights, tools and similar items. School sales may be the most prolific and popular source for tools and shop and lab items. Keep in mind that items from one area, such as lab counter tops and cabinets, work well in other areas, such as benchtops and cabinets in the wood shop.

For those using rough, green lumber from local sawmills, I suggest buying from a mill that bands its stock, after which you cover the top of the lumber with a tarp or old metal roofing and allow it to sit for a minimum of three months (six months to a year is preferable). The lumber will not be truly dry, but it will be easier to cut and nail than when truly green. Cutting and nailing green yellow pine is a working education in itself.

Consider items of used lumber. I had planned to purchase used telephone poles to build my pole building shop. The price is about 10 percent of the price of new. Again, you may have to ask around to find out who has such materials. Call the phone company's maintenance division as a start. Most pole work around where I live is done on contract, and the contractor is supposed to get rid of the poles. Other areas may work it in a slightly different manner.

Watch out for used lumber. Some is worth it, some isn't. You'll have the hassle of pulling nails before cutting, checking to see if you've left any *while* you're cutting, and being aware that you may ruin a number of saw blades on nails you miss. If you can locate an old barn, with wooden posts, joists and other materials, go ahead. I'm giving some thought to tearing down two log tobacco barns this winter. They are supposedly chestnut logs, or so I'm told. The rest is junk, but easily hauled to the dump, and the owners want the area cleared. Winter is the best time to work on this stuff, as both insects and snakes are dormant.

Sit back and think of what you need. Think of who carries the things you need. Think of who uses the products you need. Think of who used the items you need. Think of all the angles of buying cheaply, and then start looking. You'll be amazed at the amount of money you can save.

And it's fun. You'll meet people you'd otherwise not meet, and from there, you may get leads to other places and ways to save on constructing a freestanding shop or remodeling a basement or garage shop.

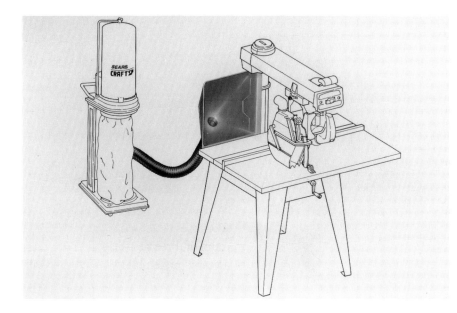

This collection kit will connect to a shop vacuum. It adapts well to other radial arm saw brands.

Courtesy of Sears.

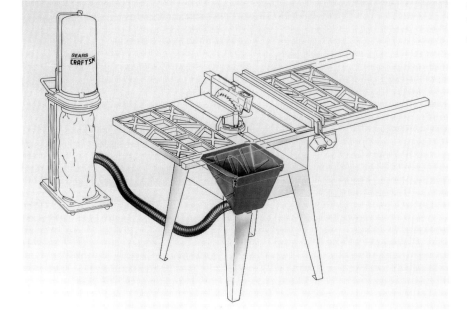

Sears' table saw dust collection setup works well on Craftsman saws and is adaptable to many other brands.

CHAPTER 4

ELECTRICAL POWER, LIGHTING AND HEAT

Electrical current needs for a woodworking shop are important. We'll start by examining what I think is important for hobby shops. I am not recommending you do your own electrical wiring unless you have considerable experience in the field. In many areas of the country it is illegal, even when done to codes, for a homeowner to do wiring. You must check your local codes and get an electrician to at least give advice.

INSPECTIONS AND PROFESSIONAL HELP

It is wisest for all do-it-yourself electricians to have a journeyman electrician inspect the completed job before having the building inspector in. That inspection prevents many problems, not the least of which is conditioning the building inspector to expect low-grade work on your site if you fail the first formal inspection. Goof it up once, and you can believe

the next inspection will be even more thorough. Building inspectors aren't in it to keep you from getting things done, but their job involves public safety and they work to make sure you will be safe in the building being erected. Pay to have it done, or make sure you do it right. Wiring is a job where neatness counts, but where design is important, too. You need correct sizes of all boxes for the numbers of conductors passing through and terminating in the boxes; the correct size wire or cable; and neat, tight connections.

I suggest you get your own copy of the National Electrical Code's most current revision. Check any wiring design you do to make sure all switch, junction and other boxes are rated for the number of wires passing through. Make sure all cable and wire are at least of the size recommended and all circuits are of correct design, too. You should have no more than eight outlets, for example, on any 110-volt, 20-ampere circuit.

Wiring must be planned and installed to suit your needs, not mine, and not those of your pal down the road. Certain commonalities hold true, but there are often major differences. If you have all 220-volt stationary tools, you'll need more 220-volt circuits than the four or five I plan to install. If you plan never to use 220-volt tools, you can probably have just one such circuit. Sooner or later you'll find a need for such a circuit, so it doesn't pay to wait and then have to combine two 110-volt circuits.

My descriptions here will be brief. I will present less-detailed installation instructions than many of you may like, but electrical wiring is a complex subject and one that requires more detailed treatment than can be supplied in a single chapter. I suggest you work with a local electrician or with a good instructional manual or code book if you have some experience and training. The wiring setups covered in this chapter are not suitable for industrial, three-phase applications. For home, hobby and most small production shops, three-phase electricity provides no benefits whatsoever. There are design difficulties as well as differing opinions on what kind of setup works best with starters, wiring and so on. It simply isn't worth the cost of hiring a journeyman industrial electrician to lay out and install a system that offers no special benefits.

You may be wiring a garage or part of a basement and need only two or three new circuits. Or you may wish to wire in a subpanel off your main service entry panel. Both are possible and practical, assuming an up-to-date service entry panel.

SERVICE ENTRY

Because it's the beginning of the circuits in your house, the service entry panel is the best starting place to discuss your wiring. Service to most residences and small shops with independent service panels and meters begins at the service entry head.

Service Entry Heads

The service entry head is the device by which electricity is transferred to the house from the pole or other power company terminal. You will find a minimum ground clearance for the service drop as it goes to the service entry head, usually 10', depending on your local code requirements. (Local code information always supersedes mine.) You supply enough wire of the appropriate size to allow a drip loop—about 12" extra, minimum. A 100-ampere service requires #3 copper conductors. With fewer than six branch circuits, you can get by with a 60-ampere service. My recommendation is that you don't try.

The service head must be within 24" of the point of attachment for the incoming service cable, which is an assembly of wires. The service head must have a crooked neck with the openings downward. Each wire will be run through an individual opening in the service head seal. Ground wires may be bare or insulated. For a 200-ampere service, you'll need to use #1 copper conductors. Local codes may be more generous with the 200-ampere service.

The service entry head is attached to the structure, usually at a cable end, and a rigid conduit is dropped to the meter. The final line drop into the house is behind or below the meter head and enters the service entry panel from an appropriate spot.

Service Entry Panels

This is where your circuitry array starts. The service entry panel holds all the circuit breakers for the entire shop. Subpanels serve the same purpose; they are fed by your existing service panel. Keep the service panels about chest high, and leave a minimum of 30" of access around the panel. More is better, because the access must be maintained so that later

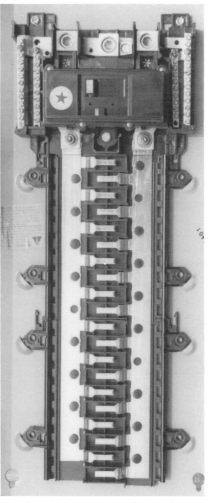

This is a 200-ampere main service entry panel, with main breaker installed and ready to hang.

This closer shot shows the buss bar and cable hook-ups.

needs can be safely met. The 30″ working distance allows you to work around and on the panel without making contact with possible conductors.

The wires enter the panel with the black wire attached to the power buss and the white wire to the neutral buss. The grounding wire—bare, green, or green stripes on white—also attaches to the neutral buss. Do the job neatly, as already noted. Strip no more insulation than is necessary, and trim it off neatly. Most indoor cable has brown paper separator inside, and sloppy electricians may leave it hanging. Bend cable to fit around corners and at right angles going into the buss bars, instead of just slopping it across the interior spaces of the panel. Trim off all excess insulation and separator paper. Do not stretch the wire tight; leave some slack inside the panel.

Most service entrance panels come with a fitted and proper main circuit breaker installed. The brand name of the panel is of importance for a couple of reasons, not the least of which is the quality of the product. Pick a name noted in the field. But you also need to know the brand name and model number of your service entrance panel to buy the correct circuit breakers for that panel. Different brand breakers attach to the panel in slightly different ways, though the technique is similar for most.

When you attach circuit wires to the circuit breakers, attach the black wire to the circuit breaker and the white and green (or bare) wires to the neutral buss or bar. That's for a 110-volt circuit. For a 220-volt circuit, attach either two black wires or a black and a red wire to the circuit breaker,

and attach the white wire to the neutral bar. You will only have a black and a red wire in the same cable if it is a three-wire cable. Most cable is classed as two-wire with ground, and with black, white and bare wires. The breaker then tilts and snaps into its place on the panel, you punch out the insert on the panel's face, and you can apply power to the circuit.

The circuit breaker is the last item hooked up when you install a new circuit. It is the first item cut off, or removed, when you work on an old circuit. *Never* work on a powered circuit.

You will work near power in the service entrance panel, and it is partly for this reason I recommend you gain some experience, or have an experienced electrician at least advising you, when wiring a shop, (or anything else, for that matter).

CIRCUITS

Two primary types of circuit are needed for the hobby woodworking shop: the lighting circuit and the appliance circuit.

Lighting Circuits

Lighting circuits carry electricity to your lights. I recommend always splitting lighting circuits so that any room has two or more such circuits. This may be even more important in a shop than in a home, for if you blow a light circuit breaker and the machinery keeps running, you can be in considerable trouble. If you have two rows of fluorescent lights in the shop, one on each side, make sure one row is on one circuit and the other is on another. It takes lot of fluorescent bulbs to pull down a lighting circuit, so you can add a second story to each side of lights and still have plenty of

power to spare. Lighting circuits are wired with #14 cable and use 15-ampere circuit breakers. There is no real reason to place either ground fault circuit interrupters or surge protectors on such circuits.

For those who don't often use the formula, a 15-ampere, 110-volt circuit lets you use up to 1,650 watts of power:

$$\text{Power or Watts} = \text{Volts} \times \text{Amperage}$$

That's a lot of any kind of light bulbs, which is why a single circuit is all that's usually recommended for lighting.

Small Appliance Circuits

Small appliance circuits provide a different service. In a home, they provide 20-ampere service to non-dedicated circuits. They offer circuits for microwave ovens, refrigerators and appliances. These are wired with #12 cable and should have both surge protection and ground fault circuit interrupters. You will use both lightweight stationary and heavyweight portable tools on these circuits, so you want as many as you can get. According to code, you can wire in as many as eight receptacles per circuit. Try it with six per circuit first. While you'll seldom run two tools at a time in such circuits, you may find you're running an air compressor and a router, or another pair of tools, on the same circuit from time to time. That's no real difficulty, unless you get double starting surges from the motors, at which point the breaker pops. It's nice to have extra circuits, with fewer outlets on each.

My suggestion here is that you leapfrog the receptacles, running two circuits along each wall, alternating receptacles from each circuit. To add some versatility, run a third circuit above the other two. For residences, the National Electrical Code requires an outlet every 12'. It is expressed differently, stating that no point along a horizontal line on a wall shall be more than 6' from an outlet, but that's how it works out. Any receptacles or outlets 5½' above the floor level are additional. You should have no problem with such a requirement, since any sensible shop construction, using my leapfrog method, should have an accessible outlet (receptacle) every 3' along the top of any bench, or along any wall, at least 18" above floor level. Space it out to 6', if you wish, but no further. With receptacles spaced any more than 6' apart, the tangle of heavy duty extension cords can compromise safety.

Regardless of what kind of wiring you do, you'll need extension cords. Do not ever use any extension cord with less than a #12 rating (up to 25' and 12 amperes). If the extension cord is longer than 50', use a #10. You'll probably have to make your own.

In areas where wall benches are used, all circuits must be placed so as to be accessible above or alongside the benches. It's much easier on the back, the nerves, and your general level of irritation to place all circuits a minimum of 18" up the wall from the floor. I'd rather have outlets at eye level than floor level.

Special outlets are available for 20-ampere circuits only. These have a T-tab on one side of the receptacles and must not be used for 15-ampere circuits.

You may, if you choose, run one or two 15-ampere general circuits around and above the benches. If you do, the above receptacles become es-sential for the 20-ampere circuits so you know what kind of circuit you're plugging lamps or tools into.

Most shops have supporting poles. Place receptacles on such poles or posts, using conduit to protect the cables.

You should also add outdoor receptacles. Almost all of us have the experience of needing to work on something outdoors—an oversize project, or one that has too much mess (fumes, paint, paint remover, etc.)—and to have to run heavy-duty extensions all over the place. Make extensions an unusual sight in your shop.

Tool Requirements

For those bigger tools you want 220 volts, usually on a 30-ampere circuit breaker. Your woodworking shop can become quite a 220-volt site if you wish. Tools are available using 220-volt electricity, but these would be tools you may find second-hand that were used professionally. Tools available with 220 include table saws, radial arm saws, planers, jointers, shapers and air compressors. Specialty tools may also use 220 volts, as may some routers and similar tools based on European patterns. Always make sure the tool is based on European patterns instead of made for use with European circuitry, which is usually 50 cycle, versus the 60 cycle we use in the United States and Canada.

Generally, any tool that requires much more than 15 amperes at 110 volts will change over to 220 volts, where the amperage load is reduced

A 220-volt, 30-ampere circuit breaker.

by 50 percent. That is, a table saw that has a motor that runs on 20 amperes at 110 volts (2,200 watts) will require only 10 amperes at 220 volts to produce the same power. A 30-ampere, 220-volt circuit, the most common size for residential and small shop use, with 50-ampere breakers, such as those used for ranges, allows 6,600 watts of power. The 50-ampere unit allows a whopping 11,000 watts. In practical terms, that means larger, lower rpm motors. Under 10,000 rpm, saws, planers and similar tools can be run, up to about five horsepower. This contrasts with a limit of 1½ to 2 horses with high torque units on 110 volts.

Most circuit breakers for 220 volts are also physically twice the size of single pole 110-volt breakers, and they take two spaces in service entrance panels. Make sure you have enough room in your plan. In a forty-space panel, five such breakers take ten spaces, leaving thirty for other uses.

Your shop needs at least twice as many 20-ampere 110-volt breakers as it needs 220 breakers, so you can figure on another ten spaces going there. For 15-ampere breakers, figure another three to five spaces, depending on your lighting and light-duty needs.

A minimum service entrance panel size for a moderately large hobby shop needs to have thirty spaces. Forty is better because it allows more for possible future needs.

Individual and immovable tools — table saws, radial arm saws, planers and air compressors — may require separate disconnects. In most cases a heavy-duty receptacle is used and the disconnect (switch box) isn't needed. Again, check with your local

building inspector.

My 200-ampere service panel is getting a full load now. There are, already, ten of the 20-ampere and five of the 30-ampere, plus at least three of the 15-ampere breakers to be settled in. There's a complex formula for all of this, involving the percent of use each circuit is expected to have, with much of the factoring dependent on things that don't truly affect a woodworking shop. A kitchen range requires 8,000 watts on any 12,000 watt or under combination of surface burners and ovens. For each kilowatt above 8,000, you add 400 watts.

For small appliance and laundry circuits, allow 1,500 watts per circuit. This is actually an overly generous allowance for the 2,400-watt rating possibility of such 20-ampere circuits (actual wattage is only 2,200 on 110 volts but is 2,400 on 120 volts.) The voltage depends on your locality and is variable from minute to minute. Up north, I always used 120 and 240 volts, while in Virginia I use 110 and 220, primarily because that's how my local electrician friends describe it in each place.

Lighting

Lighting takes a demand factor of 3 watts per square foot, which is fairly modest. I like to allow two full circuits for nothing else but fluorescent ceiling lights, plus another couple of 15-ampere circuits for general lighting. Most 15-ampere circuits allow 3-watt lighting of more than 550 square feet, so four circuits for a total of 2,000 square feet is about right for shop use, too. My difference is the recommendation that you split the circuits so that any one room of the shop, if it's a multiroom shop, has at

least two lighting circuits. If you have a single room shop, make sure the lights are on two separate circuits. The circuits then can go on and provide lights for someplace else.

In residences, you can apply a load rating system that is a bit simpler than trying to figure totals as above, and then add in load factors. With shops, you may find you absolutely must go with this kind of figuring, because anything else finds you searching out 400-ampere service entrance panel sources when all your heavy tools are added up. That is, figure the lighting at 3 watts per square foot and small appliance circuits at 1,500 watts. Figure one large tool circuit at 1,500 watts. Then list all your tools at full load ratings. If the tools aren't rated in watts, you can simply multiply the volts in your system (110 or 120) times the ampere rating listed on the tool. Add all this up, and apply a 100 percent load rating to the first 10,000 watts and a 40 percent rating at the remaining load.

Talk to your local building inspector about the types of loads you expect from various tools, and see what is acceptable locally. You may be allowed to take lighter loadings on your small appliance circuits. Obviously, a one-person shop with two table saws, two radial arm saws, spray equipment, a planer, a jointer and similar tools won't have everything operating at once. In fact, seldom will more than two tools even idle together. But it makes good sense to allow for friends or family wanting to work with you, and you may need their help on occasion. There may then actually be three or four larger tools in operation at the same time, with an air compressor in the background, its motor kicking in only

From left to right: a 20-ampere, 110-volt circuit breaker; a 15-ampere, 110-volt circuit breaker; and a 30-ampere, 220-volt circuit breaker.

when enough air is bled off to require the tank to be refilled.

In almost every instance, a 100-ampere service entrance panel will be enough for current uses, but check local codes. They may force you to a 200-ampere unit. There's not a lot of room for expansion with the 100-ampere panel, and there's none at all with the 60-ampere type.

SUBPANELS

If subpanels hold more than six circuit breakers, they may require their own circuit breaker corresponding to the main breaker on your service entrance panel. A maximum of six devices, or circuit breakers, is usually figured as being fused off the main service panel. Subpanels are protected with breakers at the main panel buss bar. The 60-ampere circuit breaker is in the main service entrance panel and allows the attachment of six more circuit breakers, or six more circuits, in the subpanel. That's a net gain of four circuits. This was needed because this service entrance panel is not a popular style. It is also old. Consequently, the buss bar was not long enough for additions to the panel.

For small shops, this 60-ampere, six-circuit array may be sufficient. Lighting may already be in place, so those circuits don't need to be added. All you need do is wire in the tool circuits.

59

WIRE AND BOXES

For almost all hobby shop wiring jobs, you will use #14 two wire with ground indoor cable, or #12 two wire with ground. Both have a black power wire, a white for neutral and usually a bare ground. The 14-gauge wire, the smaller, is used on 15-ampere circuits, and the 12-gauge wire is used on 110-volt, 20-ampere circuits, or circuits up to 30 amperes in 220. You may also use #12 three wire for the 220, which will have a white neutral and two power leads, one black and the other either brown or red.

Romex wire is fine for wiring inside walls, above ceilings, etc. For exposed wire, it should be run in conduit—either plastic or galvanized steel. Both are easy to find, and the plastic is exceptionally easy to work. The metal requires a tubing bender, a tool that's not expensive if you use it often, but it is expensive for just a single use.

A number of different junction, switch and utility boxes are apt to prove useful in wiring any shop. Junction boxes are made in a wide array of sizes and shapes, but the most commonly used are round, octagonal or square boxes. At no time do you ever join wires outside a junction box or add a switch or fixture without its own box. Splices are made using wire nuts. These are sized to the wire in the cable and are screwed on to the stripped wire ends making a sturdy, insulated connection.

While there should be no problem with pass-throughs, check current National Electrical Code regulations to make sure the size box you are using is sufficient for the number of wires in it. The cubic-inch capacity of

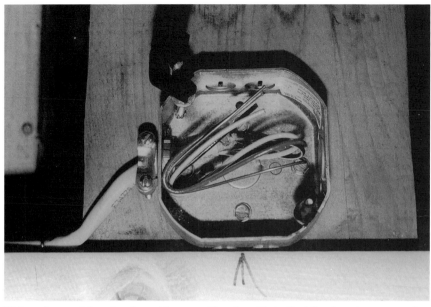

This octagonal box is placed for a ceiling fan. Note that the box is screwed into a section of 2″ × 8″ bridged between two ceiling joists.

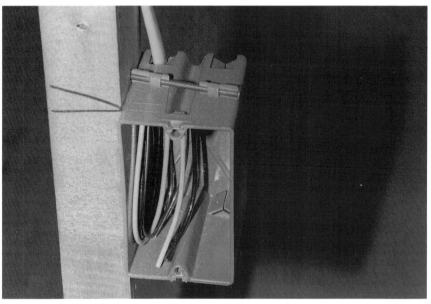

A standard single receptacle plastic wall box. Note the steel staple used to hold cable in place.

the box determines the number of wires that may be joined in that box. Usually, it's far more than you or I will ever care about, but in cases where a very shallow switch or junction box is used because of wall depth, you may find that you have a problem.

Both unprotected cable and con-duit must be supported at points during runs. Conduit is usually required to be supported within 3′ of every box, fitting or cabinet, and at intervals not more than 10′ in runs. Cable is *not* properly installed with steel staples, though for one reason or another about half the building inspectors I know will pass it. There are

Forty-eight-inch fluorescent tube lighting, backed by incandescent fixtures.

nonmetallic, usually nylon or another plastic, straps between two nails that are properly used to support cable. These must occur at the correct intervals of not more than 4½' and within 12″ of the entrance to boxes and fixtures.

Cable going into boxes and fixtures will also be held by cable clamps. Bend cable gradually. Give it a radius of at least 6″ and you're far less likely to damage the wires than if you give it a hard 90-degree bend over 1″ or so.

Wiring a shop is a fairly complex job. I'd suggest that you decide what you want in the way of receptacles and lights, and have an electrician do the actual work. If you decide to do it yourself, be careful, talk to your building inspector, and make sure you follow the most recent National Electrical Code.

LIGHTING THE SHOP
Shops have different lighting needs for different areas. There's nothing like making a job easy, but proper shop lighting isn't an easy job.

Whatever kind of shop you have, the first need is for a soft, nonglaring light from the ceiling. I find this works best with fluorescent lights, either 4' or 8' long tubes. I dislike the color of the light that those give, but the actual light is soft and nearly glare-free, something that cannot be said for most inexpensive forms of overhead incandescent lighting.

Tool Needs
You also need to think about the lighting needs of individual tools. Some, like the planer or the shaper, work fine with general light. Detail work requires more light, as close to shadow-free as possible. That means

working lights so they're either directly overhead the tool, or so they come in from two or more sides to eliminate the shadows formed by other lights. Workbenches, radial arm saws, lathes and table saws are prime examples here.

Other tools need specific lights, right at the work, almost on the work surface, allowing you to pay very close attention. Drill presses, scroll saws and band saws are often supplied with table-mounted lights as standard equipment or options. Drill presses sometimes even have the light built into the underside of the drill, as do some band saws. Where such lights aren't supplied, you might consider picking up a sturdy gooseneck light.

Work with the lighting until it is nearly shadow-free, while keeping it soft enough to remain glare-free. Harsh light, such as that supplied by uncoated 200-watt incandescent bulbs, can be really rough on the eyes over a short period of time. My erstwhile basement shop was lighted with incandescent fixtures except over two workbenches. The 200-watt coated bulbs gave me some severe eyestrain problems after a few weeks and reduced my time in the shop by at least 40 percent.

Lighting in Finishing Areas
The change in lighting comes in the finishing areas, oddly enough. To get a smooth, scratch-free finish, you need to get an angle on the surface and check for smoothness. The same holds true when applying layers of clear finish. You need to make sure all areas are covered; and glare-free, soft, shadow-free lighting just doesn't do the job.

For best results in finishing areas,

I'd suggest two of the fairly new stand-mounted halogen floodlights, set at right angles to your eyes, and at about a 15- to 30-degree angle to the surface of the work. That gives just the right kind of light to let you see whether there are scratches. The lights are easily portable for ready movement around the work, from the sanding area to the finishing area.

HEATING THE SHOP

Heating a woodworking shop is a nuisance. The best deal I ever had was a rental shop that contained the oil furnace for stores overhead. It cost me nothing and supplied more than sufficient heat in clean form.

Like all heat sources that are actually fired (using open flame), the furnace limited my winter finishing chores. The same holds true of wood heat and gas furnaces. This leaves heat pumps, electric baseboards and electric furnaces as safe methods of heating a shop during those times when you apply finishes with volatile solvent bases. That's another argument for changing over to one or more of the various water-based finishes. Heating is a problem for freestanding and garage shops, but less so for basement shops. The basement shop is apt to be sufficiently heated from the furnace for the house. With this arrangement, your only need is care in applying finishes or other substances that are likely to prove volatile. It sounds a bit odd, but the major concern in heating a woodworking shop is more apt to be the type of finishing you do than anything else.

Cutting Costs

Cost is always a factor, and one I've worked to defeat in many ways.

Wood heat is a superb way to defeat higher costs, though both wood and wood stoves have gone up in price in recent years. Insurance companies now inspect wood heat installations to see that they're safe, and the local building inspection office charges a fee for a building permit for such installations.

The cheapest heat source to install is electric baseboard. It is simple and inexpensive to install, and old units in good condition are readily available. It is also the most costly heat to feed, though that may not be a major problem in a workshop that is only heated part time.

Forget electric furnaces. They're too costly and may be hard to find. Still, it's possible you'll find a used one or two around, as mobile home owners discard theirs and install oil heat to reduce costs.

Oil stoves and furnaces provide excellent heat sources and are relatively low cost, in terms of Btu per hour output. Large oil stoves serve as well as furnaces in shops that are pri-

marily open space. The same holds true of gas heaters and furnaces, though gas furnaces tend to be a bit more costly. In both cases, we're talking of hot air heat.

Construction-style space heaters that look like torpedoes are supremely handy, but they cannot be used in an unventilated space because they are unvented and gulp huge amounts of air for combustion. These run on kerosene, are moderate in price, and can be wheeled to other cold areas if needed. However, a window or door must be left open when they're in use.

Do not use catalytic burners or other types of unvented kerosene heaters. They tend to turn out too little heat for you to really leave a door or window open, which creates problems when you collapse from lack of oxygen just as you get warm. Such heaters seldom turn out more than 17,500 Btu, so they aren't suitable for a structure, or room, of any size.

Use the cheapest heat you can af-

Chimney block makes a solid, safe chimney that is very easy to lay up.

Flue liner is essential. It is code required in solid fuel chimneys.

ford to install. As noted, baseboard electric heaters are cheap, but they're costly to run. Wood stoves are probably next, but they must have a super-efficient flue, and cord wood has gone out of sight in some areas, making running costs almost as high as an oil furnace. Possibly the best setup is an oil stove or a gas heater.

Figure on cutting heat off or way, way back when shutting the shop down. Most hobby shops are in use less than four hours a day, so heating costs shouldn't be huge, no matter the source of heat. Keep solid control of the thermostat or firewood stack at times when the shop isn't in use.

Storage During Low-Heat Periods

Like most of us, you'll worry about what might happen to supplies like stains, paints and varnishes when the shop freezes. Prevent those worries by finding an old, nonrunning refrigerator. Remove the condenser and other useless gear. It takes a great deal of long-term cold with no shop heat over quite a long period to freeze materials inside such a box.

COOLING THE SHOP

For economy purposes, air conditioning is almost out of the question, unless you've got a source for used units and very low-cost electricity. Big fans are your best bet for keeping sweat to a minimum.

CHAPTER 5

BASEMENT-TO-SHOP CONVERSIONS

Conversions of existing space in basements may sometimes be the only way to create a practical woodworking shop. Framing of basement partition walls can isolate areas from sawdust and sanding dust. Entry may create some problems, causing you to examine project selections with great care. You may even have to change some basement features to allow enough space for entry and exit of large projects.

Certain tool advantages exist today, including portable tools that until a few years ago were only available in stationary models. The current trend to decently made benchtop tools helps the woodworker with limited space to achieve the same results as the professional shop.

SMALL SPACE REQUIREMENTS

Multipurpose tools such as *Shop-smith* and *Total Shop* also fit into

Framing and insulation reduce noise and dust problems in basements.

Georgia-Pacific Corporation.

Finishing walls, whether gypsum wallboard or other drywall, greatly eases shop clean-up.

Georgia-Pacific Corporation.

small areas and provide many solutions to limited shop space, often at a surprisingly low price. With benchtop tools, there's less of a differential in price for the basic tools than there was some years ago. Multipurpose

tools offer advantages for small shops and limited budgets.

If I had to work in a small shop area, I'd select the benchtop tools I consider to be the most useful. My first choice would be a table saw, on a stand with wheels. Next would be a band saw, a 4″ jointer, and a 4″ × 6″ belt/disc sander, followed by a grinder, a 15″ or 16″ scroll saw, and an 8″ drill press.

PLANNING ON PAPER

With space conservation in mind, you may begin working on your basement. Start with graph paper, drawing board or drawing program on a computer. Measure the basement carefully, taking note of things such as doglegs, lally columns, windows, current lighting and outlets. Make a rough drawing, with rough dimensions, and determine the basic area that you can allow for woodworking.

For greatest efficiency in living, as well as in working, close off the woodworking shop from the rest of the house as well as possible. That may mean installing a partition with a door, or simply installing a door.

INSTALLING PARTITION WALLS

Partition walls in such spaces are not installed in quite the same manner as they are in other areas. With a regular wall or partition in an area that has no present ceiling, you build the wall on the floor and tip it into place. In a basement, you first take note of any pipes and wires running along under the joists. You next construct the wall without its sole plate, place the sole plate, and then set the constructed wall in place on the sole plate, setting each stud on its mark. The entire job is eased if you run a slightly diagonal 1″ × 4″ brace across the wall to keep studs from spreading too much. Nail at each stud, with a 10d nail driven in most of the way, but leaving at least ½″ sticking out so that it can be pulled easily to remove the brace

On a bench, a benchtop saw is a wonder. Build a wheeled stand, and it's even more useful.

when the wall is finally up.

As is always the case, use a double top plate on partitions and a single sole plate. If the basement floor is concrete, use cut masonry nails or other concrete anchors to hold the sole plate. Mark for each stud, placing studs on 24″ centers. The simplest way to do this is to measure from the edge of the sole plate, or the top plate, and mark a straight line down, using a combination square set at 3½″ depth, at 25½″. Mark to

the edge side of that line, and you have a 24″ center for your second stud. At the edges, mark in 1½″ and use the combination square to draw a line at that point. Place an X, in pencil, to the edge side of the line in both cases, marking where the stud end will go. Continue pacing down, measuring 24″ on center and marking the penciled X where every stud end will fall. Match the top plate to the sole plate. This is most easily done by continuing the sole plate

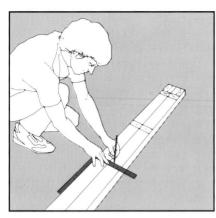

Lay out sole and top plates together for accurate fit.

Georgia-Pacific Corporation.

Make any basement partition wall 1″ shorter than floor to ceiling distance, tip into place, plumb and wedge tightly. Then nail.

Georgia-Pacific Corporation.

Door headers are framed in this manner. To make the headers, sandwich ½″ plywood between 2″ × 8″ stock— that gives a 3½″ thick header that will fit exactly with the 3½″ wide 2″ × 4″s.

mark up ¼″ or so onto the edge of the 2″ × 4″, then placing the top plate on the sole plate, marking the top plate, and using the combination square to draw the line and mark the required X. This sounds like a lot of extra work, but it saves a lot of mistakes and problems. Do this with each and every sole plate and lower top plate.

Measure and cut studs and attach to the top plate by nailing through it into the stud end. Once that's done, nail on the second top plate, place the brace, and tip the assembled wall into place. You may toenail the studs to the sole plate, or you may use framing anchors. If you don't have a lot of experience toenailing, the second method is the easiest. You can get around your lack of toenailing experience by starting the toenails before tipping the wall into place, and then finishing nailing after the wall is in place. Jam your foot against the stud on the side opposite the nails to keep the angle nailing from causing it to skitter away from its proper place. Get the nails in at a near correct angle, about 45 degrees, because too shallow an angle will have two

results, one of which is painful, as one or more nails is driven into your instep. The other result is a weak wall. The illustration presents another option, and one that works well.

FINISHING CONCRETE WALLS

For concrete basement walls, block or poured, you have a couple of choices. You may simply paint the walls with a good grade of concrete paint, or you may furr out the walls and insulate and cover them with paneling, other drywall or pegboard.

Furring strips go on easily, usually with cut masonry nails and a bit of construction adhesive. Place them on 24″ centers. You may insulate between furring strips if you wish, using a foam board insulation the same thickness as the furring strips. You may also add a vapor barrier to the warm side of the installation. Always install vapor barriers on the heated side of insulation.

After that, install paneling or other drywall as you would in any installation, nailing according to manufacturer's directions.

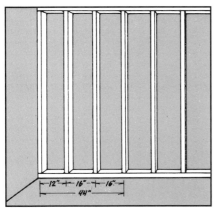

Vertical studs or furring may be used.
Georgia-Pacific Corporation.

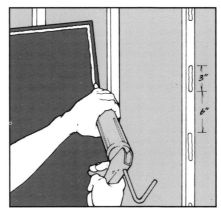

Install wallboard as shown.
Georgia-Pacific Corporation.

A Furring Method

For an optional furring method, used primarily when installation calls for narrower planks instead of large sheets of material, nail up furring strips horizontally on 16″ or 24″ centers.

To place furring strips plumb, use a chalk line with a plumb bob attached. The case on most chalk lines can be used as a plumb bob.

Mark the 24″ centers high on the wall, and drop a line from that point.

Make allowances for all electrical wiring as you place furring strips. When furring strips cross over or are cut out around cable, you must protect that cable with steel plates. Most building supply stores carry them for a few cents each. Surface wiring on concrete walls must be protected with conduit, either plastic or metal.

Keep a careful check on plumb as you shim out rough walls.
Georgia-Pacific Corporation.

Continue to check on plumb.
Georgia-Pacific Corporation.

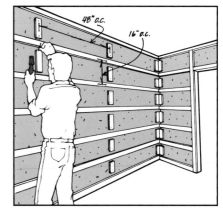

Furr walls and shim to plumb on 16″ horizontal centers, with nailer blocks on 48″ centers. Use 1″ × 2″ (¾″ × 1½″) furring strips or ½″ × 1½″ CDX plywood strips.
Georgia-Pacific Corporation.

CEILINGS

Ceiling installations in basements vary. A drop ceiling is a popular ceiling for a basement. You can use insulated 1″ tiles. Insulation shines a bit in preventing extremes of sound from rising. The floor thumps come through pretty well from upstairs to down, but the reverse isn't true. Certainly you can hear a router or table saw, but the piercing edge seems to have been peeled off. In any case, check out different ceiling materials at a local supplier, and follow the manufacturer's directions for installations. There are many systems and methods of installation. Most are fairly simple, including drop ceiling installation, requiring little more than care in measuring and installation of the original support strips.

FLOORS

Most basement floors are concrete, and concrete can create floor problems. They are not the greatest for woodworking shops because they're hard on feet and legs, hard on dropped tools, and not at all nice to projects that fall during assembly or at other times. Still, concrete beats pounded dirt, and it can be covered with any material. In any shop, you should get the antifatigue mats to give your feet, legs and back some support.

The easiest job is to just paint the concrete floor and get a few of the mats. This way the floor is easy to

Stairs may be totally enclosed in this manner to help prevent dust infiltration.

Georgia-Pacific Corporation.

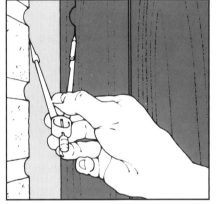

Use a compass to trace irregular surfaces onto wall board and cut with coping or scroll saw.

Georgia-Pacific Corporation.

Lally columns may be enclosed, as may metal beams.

Georgia-Pacific Corporation.

Cut out for electrical boxes. Coat the lips of the box with paint or chalk and tilt the already cut wall panel against the box. That marks the back of the panel, so you can drill all four corners and mark to cut on the front.

Georgia-Pacific Corporation.

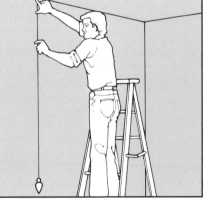

Use plumb bob or level to assure plumb of the all-important first panel.

Georgia-Pacific Corporation.

A vapor barrier helps control basement moisture.

Georgia-Pacific Corporation.

clean and, if stained, can just be re-painted. Another solution is to lay sheet vinyl or tile, best done by following the manufacturer's directions. If your floor doesn't pass moisture through, you may place any below-grade-rated vinyl tile or sheet with the appropriate adhesive. Some are self-adhesive, and much sheet material doesn't use adhesive. Do a good, tight job and the floor will last for decades. Before you start, place a piece of vinyl tile, or a similar-size

piece of plastic, down on the floor and leave it there overnight. If the weather is exceptionally dry, leave it a full week. Lift the plastic and check for moisture. If moisture is present, you must first lay sleepers — that is, 2″ × 4″s laid with the wide side on the concrete and nailed in place with cut masonry nails. You must use pressure-treated wood for this part of the job; it only costs about $5 to $10 extra and saves a repeat of the work five to six years down the road. After

you've laid the sleepers, then lay a wood subfloor over a vapor barrier, and come back with tile or vinyl sheet if you desire. If this happened to my basement, however, I'd either paint the floor and forget it, or I'd come back with sleepers, put down a double 6-mil vapor barrier, and use tongue-and-groove ⅝″ plywood as a finish floor, coated with satin polyurethane to resist battering.

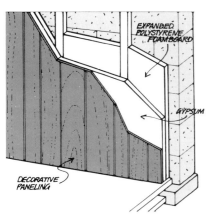

Outer walls in the basement may be insulated, if needed or desired.

Georgia-Pacific Corporation.

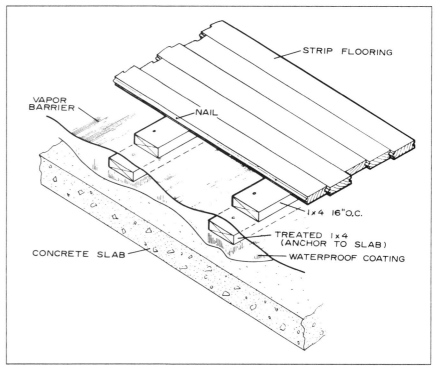

This is a base for a wood subfloor — strip is shown, but plywood is also useful — over concrete. Plywood is best under resilient tile.

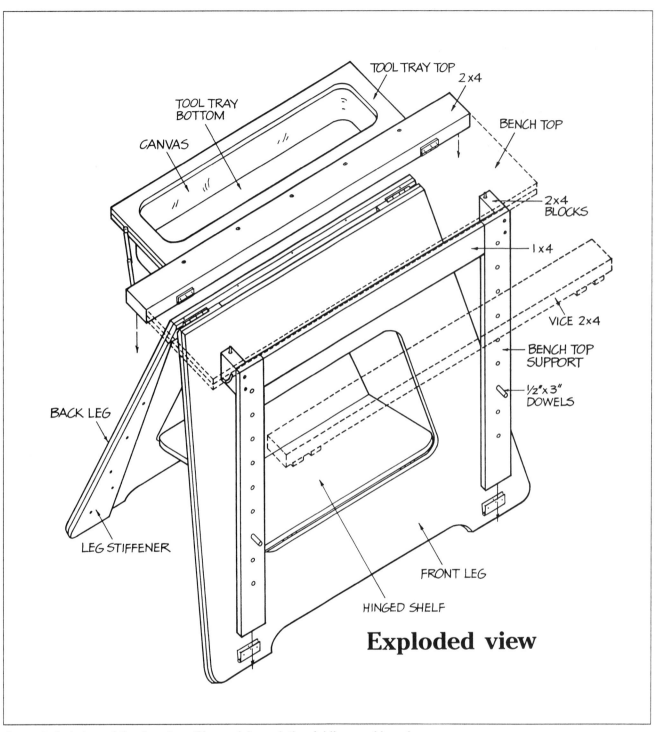

TOOL TRAY TOP

TOOL TRAY BOTTOM

CANVAS

2x4

BENCH TOP

2x4 BLOCKS

1x4

VICE 2x4

BENCH TOP SUPPORT

½"x 3" DOWELS

BACK LEG

LEG STIFFENER

FRONT LEG

HINGED SHELF

Exploded view

An exploded view of the American Plywood Association folding workbench.

Folding Workbench

Read all of the instructions before beginning this project. No matter what your space problems are, this bench can help. It is made of medium-density overlay plywood, preferably, or sanded A-B, and is light in weight and readily portable. It is easy to build, sturdy, and large enough to be useful. It offers a canvas tool tray, and you may add a vise. It is also a folding bench and can be hung on a wall.

Materials

1	sheet ⅝″ × 4′ × 8′ MDO or A-B or A-C plywood
2	2″ × 4″ × 8′ pine
1	1″ × 4′ × 40″ pine
2	1″ × 4′ × 32¾″ pine
1	1″ × 4″ × 33″ pine
2	1½″ × 2¾″ x 3″ pine blocks
2	¾″ × 1½″ × 4″ pine blocks
2	¾″ × 3″ × 4″ pine blocks
2	3″ long × ½″ dowels
1	5″ × 75″ canvas
2	6″ × 6″ angles (tie plates)
1	2″ × 18″ continuous hinge
4	2″ × 2″ hinge for shelves to legs
4	2½″ × 1½″ hinge (benchtop to 2″ × 4″, tool tray to 2″ × 4″)
2	3″ × 3″ hinge (loose pin, front leg to benchtop supports)
2	3½″ × 3½″ hinge (loose pin, leg to leg)
2	¼″ × 5″ eye bolts with nuts and washers
2	⅜″ × 4″ eye bolts (cut to size)
2	¼″ T-nuts sandwiched between benchtop and stringers, beneath eye bolt hole (see bottom view of benchtop)
2	folding lid support brackets (for tool tray)
2	pipe clamps
2	½″ screw eyes
2	1⅝″ pieces of screen door spring
5	2½″ flathead wood screws
Additional: ⅝″, ¾″, 1″, 1¼″ and 1½″ flathead wood screws, staples, aliphatic resin glue (yellow glue), wood filler, 100- and 150-grit sandpaper and finish. You may elect to paint MDO (medium density overlay), or stain and coat plywood, so the finish choice is yours.	

Tools

Tape measure
Framing square
Try square
Scribe
Carpenter's pencil
Table saw (A circular saw will also do, with good guides. If no guides are available, make your own with a couple of 3″ C-clamps and two straightedges, one 5′ long and the other 9′ long. Make sure straightedges are no more than ⅜″ thick, so no saw parts will strike and force you off line.)
Miter box
Jigsaw for curved lines
Router
10-degree dovetail bit
Cordless or corded ⅜″ drill
¼″ drill bit
⅜″ drill bit
½″ drill bit (reduced shank)
Screwdriver bits to fit screw heads used (use anticamming head types such as square drive and Phillips)
Drill bits sized to produce pilot holes for hinge screws and other screws.
Stapler
Random orbit or finishing sander
Screwdriver, with appropriate tip
Scissors (to cut canvas you may need shears)
Dikes (for cutting the metal springs)
Hammer
Nail set

Starting this project is like starting any large plywood project that doesn't involve nailing up full sheets of material. Carefully, using a framing square and straightedge, lay out all parts on the panel, following the layout drawing. Leave space for saw kerfs—usually figured at ⅛″, though new narrow kerf blades reduce this by about 50 percent. Use the first cuts to get the pieces sized for easy handling.

Where you worry about chipping, make sure you cut from the bad side with the circular saw, and the good side with the table saw—that is, the good face is down when cutting with a circular saw (and a jigsaw), and the good face is up when cutting with a table saw. This tends to dominate the way you mark the panels, because you mark the side on which the cuts are being made. It's easy enough to mark both sides, but it's a time-waster in most cases. If you're using a table saw for straight cuts, use a coping saw for curved cuts, and you can work from the same side. Actu-ally, though, those cuts need to be done after the panels have been sized with a big saw, and they may be marked later, so the cuts are readily made with the jigsaw (also called a saber saw, or bayonet saw).

You can reduce edge chipping when sawing by taping the panel, with masking tape, along the lines of the cuts.

Use scrap wood to back up where holes are drilled all the way through panels to prevent splintering at the exits.

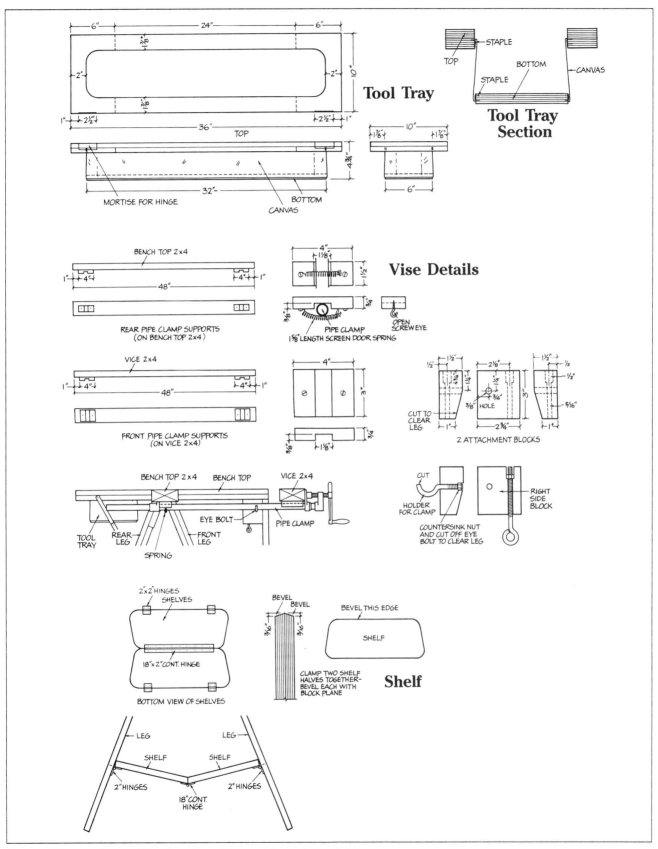

Plan and layout views of the American Plywood Association folding workbench.

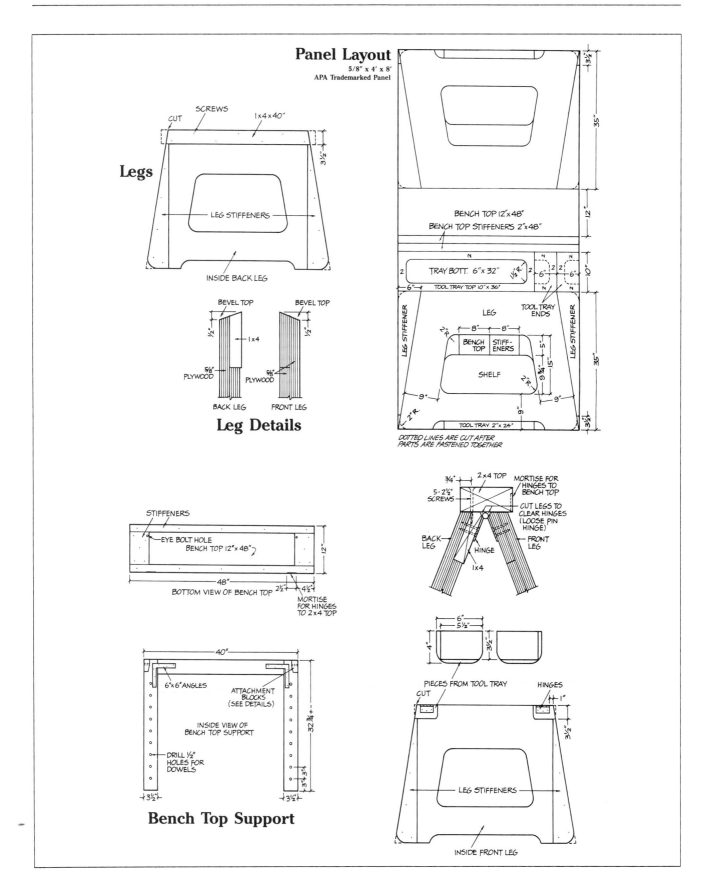

Panel Layout
5/8" x 4' x 8'
APA Trademarked Panel

Legs

SCREWS
CUT
1 x 4 x 40"
3½"

LEG STIFFENERS

INSIDE BACK LEG

Leg Details

BEVEL TOP
BEVEL TOP
½"
1 x 4
⅝"
PLYWOOD
⅝"
PLYWOOD
BACK LEG
FRONT LEG

BENCH TOP 12" x 48"
BENCH TOP STIFFENERS 2" x 48"
TRAY BOTT. 6" x 32"
TOOL TRAY TOP 10" x 36"
LEG STIFFENER
LEG STIFFENER
LEG
TOOL TRAY ENDS
BENCH TOP
STIFF-ENERS
SHELF
TOOL TRAY 2" x 24"
35"
12"
10"
35"
3½"
8"
8"
5"
15"
9¾"
9"
9"
2" R.

DOTTED LINES ARE CUT AFTER
PARTS ARE FASTENED TOGETHER

STIFFENERS
EYE BOLT HOLE
BENCH TOP 12" x 48"
12"
48"
BOTTOM VIEW OF BENCH TOP
2½"
4½"
MORTISE
FOR HINGES
TO 2 x 4 TOP

¾"
2 x 4 TOP
MORTISE FOR
HINGES TO
BENCH TOP
5 - 2½"
SCREWS
CUT LEGS TO
CLEAR HINGES
(LOOSE PIN
HINGE)
BACK
LEG
FRONT
LEG
HINGE
1 x 4

Bench Top Support

40"
6" x 6" ANGLES
ATTACHMENT
BLOCKS
(SEE DETAILS)
INSIDE VIEW OF
BENCH TOP SUPPORT
DRILL ½"
HOLES FOR
DOWELS
32¾" +-
3" 3"
3½"
3½"

6"
5½"
4"
3½"
PIECES FROM TOOL TRAY
CUT
HINGES
1"
3½"

LEG STIFFENERS

INSIDE FRONT LEG

Clean up edges with 100-grit sandpaper.

Cut all nonplywood parts next, and drill holes for the ½″ × 3″ dowels in the uprights. Attach the 2″ × 4″ blocks at the top of the benchtop supports. Install 6″ × 6″ angles on the benchtop supports, making sure all angles are square. Hinge these supports to the lower front leg, at distances on the drawing. Attach the benchtop to the supports and locks, and staple the tool tray canvas to the tool tray and tool tray bottom.

Next, hinge the two leg assemblies together at their tops, after applying leg stiffeners.

Attach the bottom shelf with hinges as shown. The 18″ continuous hinge goes up the center, with 2″ hinges at the legs, all set so the shelf can fold correctly. Shelf edges need a double bevel, cutting back ³⁄₁₆″ to the material center (in thickness) on each side. You can do this most easily with a router and bit — probably about 10-degree dovetail bit will work best.

For a good fit, mortise the 2″ × 4″ and benchtop where the hinges are attached. The top is assembled as shown, with stiffeners to prevent flex.

Once assembly is complete, you can remove all hardware and sand carefully before final finish. For a painted finish, use a 100-grit sandpaper, and fill all plywood edges with wood filler. For a clear finish, fill all edges with wood putty, but use a 150-grit paper for the finish sanding: Start with 100 grit and give the whole project, including filled edges, a light sanding, and lightly sand with the finer paper. Clean up with a tack cloth, and coat with stain and finish.

Reassemble, and you're ready to work.

Vise Table and Sawhorse

While the preceding unit works nicely to help you utilize tight spaces, it's also a fairly complex project itself. This one does a similar job, and it also allows you to work outside in nice weather, with little hassle attached to cleaning up, folding up, and getting back inside when the work is done. And it's a little easier to build, though there's some metal drilling involved. The project still only uses a single sheet of plywood, plus a few other parts. The resulting pair offers large work areas — the top of the vise table is 24″ × 36″ when closed. Height is 29″, so you can work standing up. If you will be doing a lot of small work I'd suggest a stool, because 29″ is really about 5″ lower than an average-height person needs for a standing work bench. The standard is 34″, but if you measure from your palm, with arm loosely at your side and hand held horizontal, and add 3″, you'll get a pretty good custom measurement.

The American Plywood Association folding workbench.

**The folding workbench
in its storable state.**

Courtesy of American Plywood
Association.

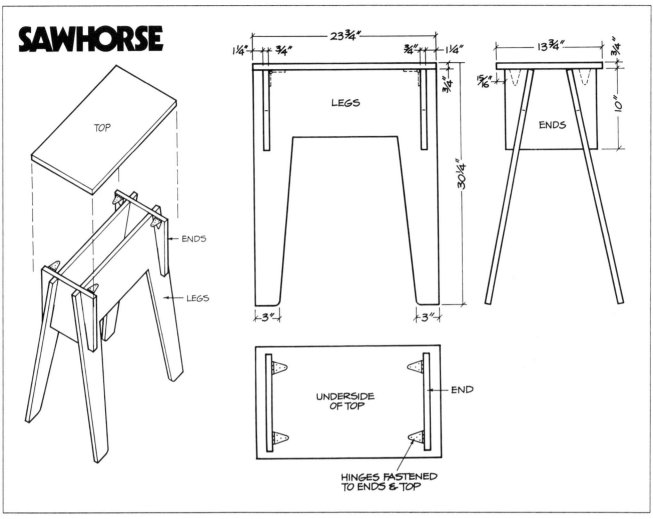

Exploded view, plan drawing and layout drawing for the folding vise table and sawhorse.

Courtesy of American Plywood Association.

Materials

1	sheet A-B or A-C exterior plywood
12	strap hinges, 1½", with screws
4	pieces angle iron, 1½" × 2"
2	pieces threaded rod, ⅜" diameter × 18"
4	nuts to fit the threaded rod
2	bolts, ¼" × 5"
2	lock nuts, ⅜" × ½" deep
20	#8 × 1¼" flathead wood screws
8	#8 × 2" flathead wood screws
8	#8 × 1¼" round head wood screws
2	carriage bolts, ¼" × 2", with nuts
4	compression pins, ⅛" diameter × 2"

Wood filler
Aliphatic glue (yellow carpenter's or woodworker's glue)
Paint or clear finish
100- and 150-grit sandpaper

Tools

Tape measure
Framing square
Try square
Scribe
Carpenter's pencil
Table saw (A circular saw will also do, with good guides. If no guides are available, make your own with a couple of 3" C-clamps and two straightedges, one 5' long and the other 9' long. Make sure straightedges are no more than ⅜" thick, so no saw parts will strike and force you off line.)
Jigsaw for curved lines
12 3" C-clamps
12 deep-throat C-clamps or deep bar clamps (at least 8" throat to reach as close to center of 24" as possible, in rows from each side and end)
Cordless or corded ⅜" drill
⅝" reduced shank wood bit
3/16" metal bit
⅛" metal bit
5/16" metal bit
7/16" metal bit
¼" tap
⅜" tap
Center punch
Screwdriver bits to fit screw heads used (use anticamming head types such as square drive and Phillips)
Drill bits sized to produce pilot holes for hinge screws and other screws.
Random orbit or finishing sander
Screwdriver, with appropriate tip
Hammer
Nail set

Start with the layout of parts on the plywood sheet. Carefully, using a framing square and straightedge, lay out all parts on the panel, following the layout drawing. Leave space for saw kerfs, usually figured at ⅛", though new narrow kerf blades reduce this by about 50 percent. This project layout doesn't have a kerf allowance, so center-saw cuts on the kerf, where there are two pieces, so the loss of material is the same on both pieces. Use the first cuts to get the pieces sized for easy handling.

Sand plywood edges smooth, and slide sawhorse ends into leg slots to check and adjust fit. Fasten the ends to the top, using the 1½" strap hinges.

Now, laminate the two tabletop sections together, using glue and clamps. Give each face (to be glued faces only, of course) a thin coating of wood glue, and line the pieces up. Clamp the outside edges so they're even, using two C-clamps on each end and four up each side, spaced about equally. Space the deep-throat clamps about the same, but reach as far into the 24" depth as possible. If you can locate the correct depth clamps, a row that reaches right to the center will be a big help; but you can get a good clamping action with 8" deep clamps. When dry, rip into two 12" wide pieces.

Build the runner channels with side and bottom plates as shown in the drawings, and fasten to the stationary section of the top, as the drawing shows. Make certain the sections are dead parallel so the sides

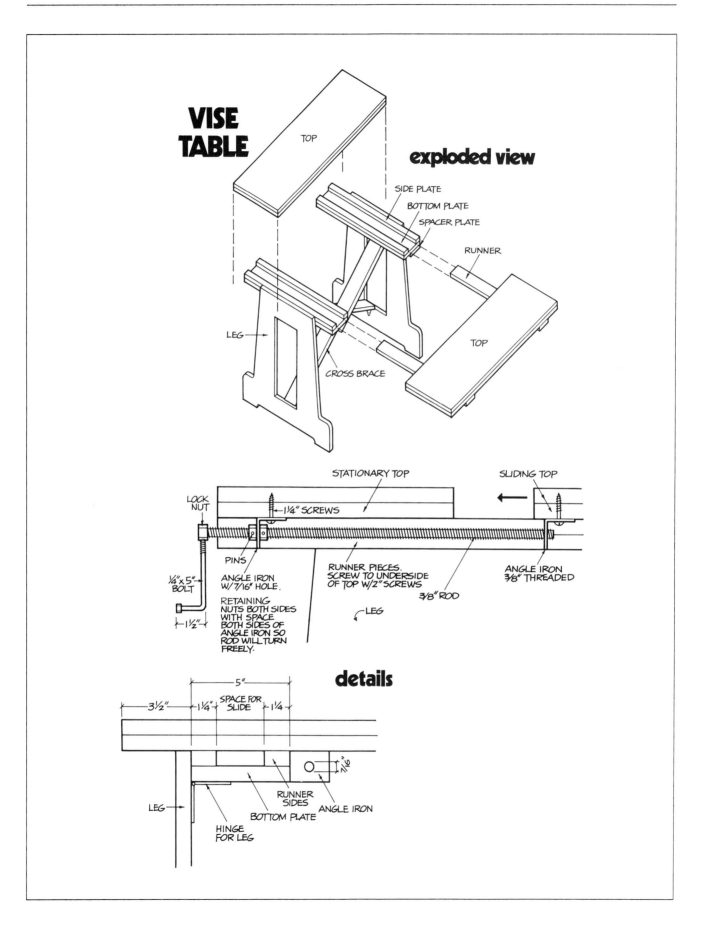

VISE TABLE

exploded view

TOP

SIDE PLATE
BOTTOM PLATE
SPACER PLATE

RUNNER

LEG

TOP

CROSS BRACE

STATIONARY TOP

SLIDING TOP

LOCK NUT

1¼" SCREWS

¼" x 5" BOLT

PINS

ANGLE IRON W/ 7/16" HOLE.

RETAINING NUTS BOTH SIDES WITH SPACE BOTH SIDES OF ANGLE IRON SO ROD WILL TURN FREELY.

RUNNER PIECES. SCREW TO UNDERSIDE OF TOP W/2" SCREWS

LEG

3/8" ROD

ANGLE IRON 3/8" THREADED

1½"

details

5"

3½"

1¼"

SPACE FOR SLIDE

1¼"

7/16"

LEG

HINGE FOR LEG

BOTTOM PLATE

RUNNER SIDES

ANGLE IRON

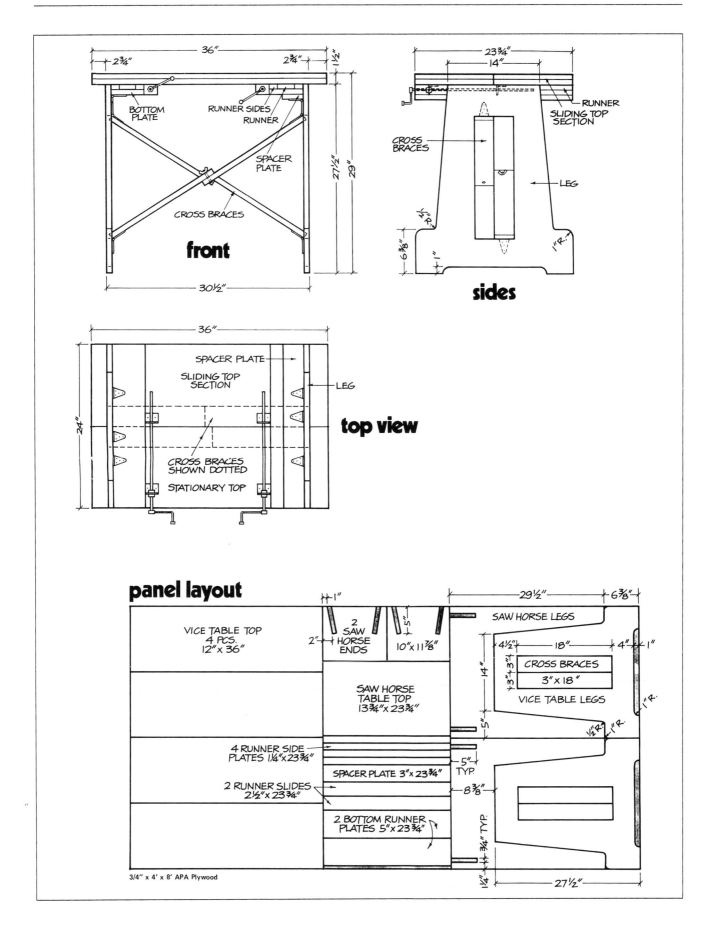

front

sides

top view

panel layout

3/4" x 4' x 8' APA Plywood

The American Plywood Association folding vise table and sawhorse.

don't bind. Use glue and flathead screws, with 2″ screws where the channel fastens to the top and 1¼″ screws where it fastens elsewhere. Attach the spacer plate using glue and 1¼″ screws. When using glue and screws, mark alignment of dry parts and drill any pilot holes with dry parts clamped. If you try to drill pilot holes in parts with glue already applied, you'll get a mess.

Place the runner slide in the runner channels and put the movable table side on top of the slides. Mark the positions of the slides on the un-derside of the movable table piece, and then use 1¼″ screws and glue, and screw slides to the movable table section as shown in the drawing. Doing it this way makes sure the unit will be free-running.

Hinge the legs to the stationary tabletop assembly, with the spacer plate on one side so the legs can fold flat. Install the hinges that hold the cross braces to the legs, with placement as shown in the end and front views. Where the cross braces overlap, drill a ⁵⁄₁₆″ hole through the braces and insert carriage bolts and wing units, which are removable for storage.

Drill a ³⁄₁₆″ hole through a lock nut and tap with a ¼″ thread. Place the nut so it acts as a handle-to-rod connector on one end on the threaded rod, and insert one of the 5″ long bolts. Bend the bolt's end to form a handle. Make the second rod up in the same manner.

Drill two ³⁄₁₆″ holes in one flange of each angle iron to take 1¼″ × #8 round head mounting screws. Center a ⁵⁄₁₆″ hole in the remaining flanges of the angle irons to be installed on the movable table section, and tap to fit the threaded rod. Center a $7/16''$ hole on the remaining flanges of the angle irons to be installed on the stationary table piece.

Using $1\frac{1}{4}''$ round head screws, fasten the angle irons beneath table sections (see drawings) flush against the inside edges of the runner channels. The $7/16''$ and $5/16''$ holes drilled should align, front to rear.

Install the threaded $3/8''$ rods and hardware as shown in the drawing. Drill $1/8''$ holes through retaining nuts and rod. Insert the compression pins to lock the nuts in place.

For woodworking, drill $5/8''$ holes in the vise tabletop. Use $5/8''$ dowels to hold a variety of shapes and sizes when using the vise table.

Remove the movable section and carriage bolts, and fill all edges with wood putty. Sand edges, and prime and paint; or finish with stain and clear finish. Reassemble, and you have your working vise table and sawhorse set ready for use.

CHAPTER 6

GARAGE-TO-SHOP CONVERSIONS

■

You would be wise to apply the lessons from the early chapters to prevent problems created by converting a garage into a woodworking shop. In general, the fact that you've got enclosed, wired and lighted space saves 95 percent of the work involved in setting up a woodworking shop.

In a garage space, materials access is seldom a problem. For those who keep vehicles in the garage, a good option is tilt-up workbenches and combination tools. Tool selection and placement have a considerable effect on ease of use of any space that is not specifically constructed for shop uses. Unless you are building a new garage, you do not have the option of selecting door and window placement, ceiling height, floor materials and similar features. You can work out all of this at low cost, if you carry out appropriate planning when selecting tools, workbenches and materials.

USE OF GARAGE SPACE

A good garage solves a lot of workshop space and construction problems. Most are simple frameworks with roof and siding; there may also be a couple of windows, some electrical power, and a light or two. The garage door is close to an ideal material and equipment portal. If the garage is attached to the house, there may be enough heat bleeding off to reduce or eliminate any need for a separate heating system. There may also already be circuits enough for a modest shop, but the odds are good you'll eventually need to install at least a 60-ampere subpanel.

Again, drawing the outline of the building's interior will help. Locate doors and windows. Decide whether the garage will ever be used for vehicular storage and work. Decide what tools will fit where and what kind of outlets you need. See if there's room and power for all. Install the electricity, pegboard and other accessories you need to complete the shop. The

fact is, most such garages offer about 450 to 600 square feet of space, sufficient for all but the largest hobby shops.

WALLS AND CEILING

Most garages will have open studs, probably open rafters and collar beams, and maybe even ceiling joists. It's up to you as to how much finishing you do. The floor is almost sure to be concrete and may demand some extreme clean-up before it will even take a coat of paint. Check with floor paint manufacturers to see what they recommend for cleaning up greasy floors. Or you may again go the sleeper route, which is probably preferable and sometimes necessary if the floor is really nasty. Get enough grease in concrete over enough years, and it cannot be properly cleaned so that paint or adhesive for various tiles will adhere.

You need to make up your mind whether you'll place a ceiling in the garage. In one sense, a ceiling is desir-

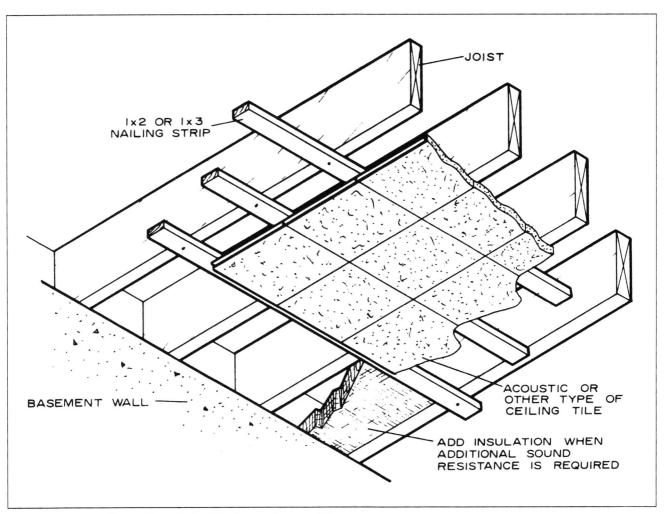

JOIST

1 x 2 OR 1 x 3
NAILING STRIP

BASEMENT WALL

ACOUSTIC OR
OTHER TYPE OF
CEILING TILE

ADD INSULATION WHEN
ADDITIONAL SOUND
RESISTANCE IS REQUIRED

Garages adapt well to ceiling tile installed over furring strips.

able. In another, it's not. Open rafters or lower members of trusses make decent storage spots for light items long enough to span at least two of the members. And there are a sufficiency of those in every woodworker's life. The ceiling is desirable because it tends to reduce heating and cooling needs, while also providing a reflective surface (if light-colored) for light. Your storage needs must be balanced against the excessive heat loss and gain you will face, plus the dust and general clutter accumulation that is always the case when open rafters are over a woodworking shop.

You also must decide whether to add drywall to the studs. Certain areas are best left open; the studs can become the source of superb storage opportunities. You may, as the enclosed drawings show, cut patterns from ¾″ plywood. Make one end 6″ deep, the other 2″, and taper the bottom to that end, with an overall length of 12″. The resulting support is nailed or screwed with at least three 8d or larger nails in a triangular pattern to the stud. You may then come down the line and cut out ¾″ plywood or regular boards to fit around the studs, or set lumber on the supports, using it as a storage and drying rack. You may also make the supports 7″ deep, taper them to 2½″

at 16″ out, and use the 12″ space in front of the studs for lumber and other storage, with or without shelves.

If you decide to place a ceiling, first insulate as local dictates make sensible. At a minimum, that's 3½″ in the walls and 6″ over the ceiling. Next, using either ¼″ waferboard or oriented strand board, cover the walls and ceiling. Currently, my office is done in waferboard with lath at 4′ intervals. The whole works is painted off-white. It looks great and is bright and cheery, so a shop will do as well. I've used waferboard in shops before and find it an easy-to-use, sturdy and low-cost way to cover

Between studs, shelving goes up quickly and is super adaptable.

Courtesy of American Plywood Association.

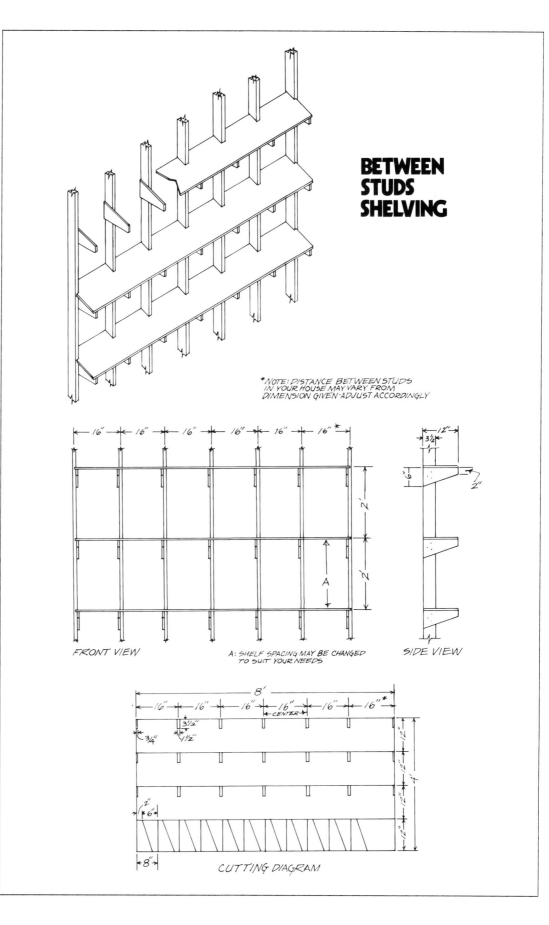

BETWEEN STUDS SHELVING

*NOTE: DISTANCE BETWEEN STUDS IN YOUR HOUSE MAY VARY FROM DIMENSION GIVEN-ADJUST ACCORDINGLY

FRONT VIEW

A: SHELF SPACING MAY BE CHANGED TO SUIT YOUR NEEDS

SIDE VIEW

CUTTING DIAGRAM

gaping spaces in walls and to cover old, deteriorating plaster walls without going to huge expense. Of course, if you prefer, you can use another type of paneling, but I know of nothing else that is as good, easy and low cost. Even in today's current high-priced sheet wood market, waferboard in ¼″ thickness is less than $8 per panel.

The panels go up quickly and are nailed at 8″ intervals on internal seams and 6″ intervals along the outside edges. You may use a few dabs of construction adhesive to make for a surer bond, but be advised you will probably never be able to remove the panels that are glued down unless you take some serious chunks out of the studs underneath.

You may build workbenches in stud walls, with only front legs for support.

The extent of the remodeling is up to you, as always, but make sure you've got sufficient circuits. Use up as much wall space as possible with pegboard or shelving. Today's garages are most often built with studs on 24″ centers, which makes for easy installation of most kinds of drywall paneling.

Attached Garages

In most instances, attached garages with a wall next to the home's living area will make everyone happier if it's filled with insulation, which will help reduce the passage of sound. However, the only way to completely prevent the passage of sound is with a second wall that is placed about 1″ in front of the first, with no solid contact between the two, and with insulation woven in to help reduce sound travel. It is seldom worth the expense and effort.

WINDOWS AND DOORS

Evaluate the location of windows and doors, and the condition of things such as overhead doors and automatic openers, when getting set to do your planning. Doors may be easily added, especially standard entry doors, up to 36″ wide, but you are probably better off not adding any windows. Windows produce glaring light and seem to do so always at the wrong time; they're also easily broken if they're too low, and most windows, including those in a garage, are too low for workshop use. Leave those that exist in place, but don't add more unless the sills are at least 54″ from the floor.

The simplest solution for double-hung windows that are too low is to cover much of the bottom with a piece of plywood, raising the wall space 12″ or more, and reducing use of the window to the top sash unit. The plywood across the bottom should be at least ⅜″ thick; it will eliminate broken panes from swinging lumber, kickbacks and similar problems. Before covering such window spaces permanently, check local codes. In most residences, ground-floor rooms are required to have a window large enough for exit of a person. Do *not* make a change without checking this first, because you may end up with a disapproved installation. If codes forbid such permanent installation, use two small butt hinges on one side and a slide latch on the other.

Permanent closing up of the bottom of a window allows you to run benches along the wall that are higher than might otherwise be the case. If a garage has windows at the level of some of those in residences, you will be limited in placing anything against

them. If such is the case, and you can't make a change by stopping up the lower half of the window, I suggest placing a tool such as a band saw or drill press in front of the window. Lathes will also fit, but there is some tendency for lathes to fling things that will break windows, so they're not the best selection here. Drill presses and band saws seldom create such problems.

That big door is a help. If you do not have an automatic garage door opener, I suggest you install one. The installation isn't particularly difficult, and the time it saves is great, especially if there's no other exterior door in the garage. I recommend that you install another exterior door, at least 32″ wide, with consideration given to a 36″ wide model. In a normally framed garage, that means removing a single stud, and framing in to take the door. To build a header, take a ½″ piece of plywood and sandwich it between two 2″ × 8″ studs. Installed across the span this will create a sturdy frame for window installation. If the framing is of rough-cut lumber, use double pieces of ½″ plywood as spacers. Use at least one jack stud under each side of the header and one cripple stud in its center, to the top plate, if the space is large enough to allow it. Make sure the sill (floor) is level and the rough framing is plumb, and insert the door unit. Nail through the door jamb sides into the framing after shimming at the lock area and elsewhere as needed for a solid installation. Install molding, and the job is done.

LIGHTING

My recommendation is to install overhead fluorescent lights. First you must evaluate the electrical system

In existing construction add sleepers and plywood or other flooring as you wish.

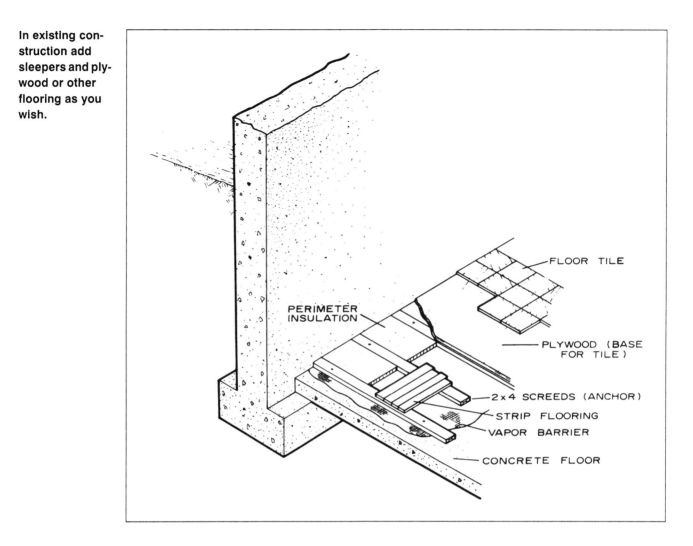

FLOOR TILE

PERIMETER INSULATION

PLYWOOD (BASE FOR TILE)

2 x 4 SCREEDS (ANCHOR)

STRIP FLOORING

VAPOR BARRIER

CONCRETE FLOOR

and work as in chapter four. Make sure you have a sufficiency of outlets in both 110 and 220, and also make sure you have a properly grounded electrical system. If you install a ground fault circuit interrupter at the first outlet in any series, you protect all the outlets following from that point. You may also add in circuit breakers of the ground fault circuit interrupter type, though they tend to be more expensive than standard breakers.

FLOORING

Evaluate the floor. Ideally, you won't have to do a thing except wash and paint the floor, or lay tile. However, many garages with poured concrete floors have a central drain, and the floor slopes toward that drain. If there is too much slope, you may need to work out some method of leveling the floor. The only effective way to do so is to install a leveled floor on sleepers. It's not the hardest job in the world, but it does take time and money.

Level the sleepers as you install them, starting from the sides of the room and working toward the center. Level all succeeding sleepers with the high ones along the walls. Install sleepers with construction adhesive and cut masonry nails, using pressure-treated pine treated to at least a .25 pound per cubic foot retention rate (not for ground contact). For

problem areas that are apt to stay wet, use .40 pressure-treated wood, and use a good vapor barrier laid directly on the concrete. Vapor barriers are made from polyethylene sheeting no less than 6 mils thick.

Install sleepers so centers are either 16" (for ⅝" plywood floor, no subfloor), or 24" (for ¾" floor, or ⅝" over board subfloor). If it's a normal installation, use a ¾" (1" nominal) sheathing lumber for subfloor; or a rough-cut 1" lumber with a ⅝" tongue-and-groove sanded B-C plywood finish floor works well. You can then either lay vinyl tile or vinyl sheet on the plywood, or you can simply coat it with a good brand of polyurethane.

HEAT AND ELECTRICITY

Heat installation in a garage may require a flue or wall vent, depending on the heat type. Connected garages typically have little need for extra heating, but you may wish to add a couple of baseboard electric units or a small wood stove. If you do add a wood stove, you must install a chimney with a solid fuel liner and have it and the rest of the installation inspected to make sure it conforms to regulations.

Connected garages also tend to offer easy access to any necessary circuitry upgrades by the simple process of adding a subpanel to a couple of unused circuit breaker spaces in the main service entry panel. Depending on the present load on the main panel, you can take off enough for six to ten circuits with little problem. The six-circuit box will not need its own circuit breaker, but will use the breakers on the main panel. For a larger subpanel, you will need a separate breaker, either 60 or 100 amperes.

TOOL CHOICES

Beyond that, working a garage up into a workshop is a job that requires little extra work, unless you plan to leave one or more vehicles inside. If you do, then it's more a matter of tool choice and the ability to move those tools into place easily when you have a job to do.

Choose benchtop tools if the garage is deep enough to allow at least a 22″ deep bench against the back wall, or tools with wheels and multiple uses. Multipurpose tools make a good selection. Check the items in your local tool suppliers' showrooms and in the catalogs available from most tool manufacturers. A good source book for tools and materials is *The Woodworker's Source Book* (Betterway Books, Cincinnati, Ohio) for up-to-date information on tool suppliers, from manufacturers and distributors to mail order houses.

CHAPTER 7

BUILDING THE FREESTANDING SHOP

F rame construction principles are the same whether you build a residence or a shop. You can generally get by with cheaper finish materials for a shop, but you must use the same depth and quality of footings, wall framing, electrical, plumbing, roofing, insulation, etc.

All construction starts with layout and design. Most building inspection offices want you to present them with rough plans before you are granted a permit. Shop structures are much simpler than residences: You don't usually add items such as bathrooms, kitchens, central air conditioning or, for that matter, central heat. Most freestanding shop heating that I've seen is done with a space heater of some sort, whether kerosene, electric, coal or wood. I would suggest, for cleanliness, that your finishing area be heated with something other than wood or coal. Finishes pose some problems during application and drying when heat with open flame is used. Water-based polyurethanes eliminate most of those problems, but they are not totally suitable for all wood finishing needs.

TOOLS

Some of the same tools used in a woodworking shop are very handy for constructing that shop. These are carpentry tools, and their selection and use is one of the factors on which your success or failure in creating a woodworking shop depends.

Carpentry tools can add more expense to any outdoor work, or they can be rational in cost and add to the enjoyment and ease with which your work is done. Efficiency and lowest possible cost within your own range of needs should be the determining factors. If you are going to drill a total of fifty holes, with none larger than about ⅜″, don't purchase a professional ½″ hammer drill at a cost of more than $300. However, if your intention is to do quality work over a period of years, the small $35 consumer drills are not the way to go. Long lasting, quality tools are expensive. As with most everything else, you get what you pay for.

Always keep one point in mind: Truly cheap tools are never a good buy. Panel saws will not cut a straight line, hammer faces are belled incorrectly and bend more nails than a sloppy carpenter. Cheap measuring tools will be inaccurate and sloppily made, squares will not be square, levels may not level correctly, and screwdrivers will not fit slots or will chip and break at the tips. Spending money for luxury tools is not always a good idea. Certain tools can be had in price ranges that vary widely, but the ultraspecial models are simply not necessary for good work (though owning them does provide a fine feeling for many people).

Hand Tools

Basic hand tools needed for any construction work include the claw hammer, the panel or hand saw, screwdrivers in various styles and types, planes, chisels, a miter box, nail sets, measuring tapes and rules, squares, levels, a brace and bit set or electric drills, and some small items that might be classed as accessories, such as stair stringer markers for framing squares.

Hammers

Claw hammers are apt to be found in almost every home, and the ones there would give most professionals the chills. Junk hammers are a waste of money. When hammer shopping, check for a clean chamfer around the face and a very slightly crowned face to allow directional control when driving nails. The entire head should be cleanly made and the claws cleanly beveled. Nail hammer heads come in two patterns, one having curved claws and the other having straight, or ripping, claws. Ripping hammers are used most often for heavier framing work and are said to be less well balanced for driving nails. You will find that for heavy framing hammers there is often no other choice. Models with head weights from 22 ounces on up to 28 ounces have ripping claws. Curved claw hammers, also known as finish hammers, offer easier gripping of nails to be pulled and a slightly better control when driving nails, so they are preferred for lighter finish work.

Handle materials range from hickory to fiberglass to solid and tubular steel. There are slight advantages to each. Wood costs less; fiberglass is easiest of all on the hand and forearm when driving nails; and solid steel handles are the strongest. The most important consideration with any hammer handle is that it is securely attached to the head, which is a feature emphasized by all the good brands.

Head weight is a personal consideration. Standard weights range from 13 ounces, primarily used for finish trim work, to the standard 16-ounce head, on up to 28-ounce framing hammers with extra handle length to provide driving power for large nails and spikes.

Faces may be plain or milled. Milled faces are only useful in hammers used for rough framing.

Handsaws

There is a good variety of handsaws available, but for most purposes only four are of use: the handsaw, the keyhole (compass) saw, the backsaw and the hacksaw (for cutting metals).

Panel saws were once the epitome of carpentry saws used for crosscutting and ripping, but things have changed. Power tools are used far more often for both of those cuts. The panel saw is now only used for small jobs and to use where electrical power is not available.

For general crosscutting use, a 10-point-per-inch blade is preferable (panel saws are widely available in 8-, 10- and a 12-point-per-inch models). Select a good model; cheap saws do not cut straight even when new. Make sure the handle contours are comfortable and the teeth are sharp.

Take a good look at the newer hard tooth and aggressive tooth patterns. Manufacturers have produced quick-cutting saws that reduce effort considerably over older chisel-tooth patterns. I still use the older patterns but find more and more of my work is being done with the varied aggressive tooth types, including the finish cut 12-tooth patterns. Keyhole saws are useful, inexpensive tools that may sometimes be part of what is called a nest of saws. They're used for notching and for cutting small openings, such as receptacle holes.

Backsaws are usually a part of hand miter boxes. Instead of a top taper as in a panel saw, the backsaw will have a flat pattern blade, with a steel or brass rib along its top to stiffen the blade, for a very accurate straight line cut. The better backsaws will be larger and stiffer, with better metal used in the blade so the teeth will hold their set and edge longer.

Screwdrivers

Screwdrivers are among the most used and most mistreated tools of all. The old slotted-head screwdriver is not gone, but it sure is slowing down these days as power drivers become ever more popular. Slotted-head screwdrivers are being replaced for most work with Phillips, square drive and other specialty heads.

Screwdrivers need to have handles that fit the hand well so that constant use doesn't result in sore hands and forearms. One that fills the closed hand is good, and the wedge-shaped models are close to ideal. The shanks and blades need to be of good metal, and the tips must be accurately machined. After that, it's a matter of matching tip size to the size of the slot (or other inset) on the screw, and applying a twisting motion.

Shank length is a matter of job requirements and preferences. It is best to use a medium-length shank, say 6" to 8", whenever possible, as these are the easiest to control. Moving into very short and very long lengths should be done only when there's no other way to do the work.

Squares and Levels

Squares of at least two types are essential to most carpentry, indoor or outdoor. The basic try square is a simple, rigid form of metal, or wood and metal. It has a 90-degree angle and might also offer short 45-degree cut across the handle base. The blade size is usually 8″ or 12″ long and will be marked, as you wish, in inch or metric measurements.

A slightly different form of the standard try square is the combination square. Combination squares have blades that slide in the handles and offer both 90- and 45-degree markings with ease, though generally with slightly less accuracy than does a good try square. The loss of accuracy is of little importance in most carpentry work.

Framing, carpenter's, and roofing squares are all versions of the same tool, a stamped L of metal with a 2″ wide blade and a 1½″ wide tongue. The square may be of aluminum or steel. Stainless steel is the best, though the heaviest, and may have ink-filled or unfilled numbers and tables. The long member makes for a good straightedge on much work, and the square is essential to many kinds of framing work, from checking square on corners to laying out rafters and stair stringers.

Levels are essential. Three types of bubble levels will cover every job likely to be required by woodshop carpentry work. The standard spirit level, at least 2′ long, is needed for leveling items such as window sills, plumbing door frames, and plumbing posts and other uprights. For doing a lot of doors, a 72″ or 78″ level is a good idea. The 9″ torpedo level does the same jobs in spots where the longer level doesn't fit. Line levels

clip on to mason's cord and provide a level over a long distance, as for the original layout of the building.

I haven't covered all the hand tools you'll need for all the jobs in this book, but I have given the basics of the most important. Items such as nail sets, specialized screwdrivers, mason's hammers and so on will make themselves known to you as you work.

Power Tools

For the basics of carpentry, you can squeeze by with only two power tools. You'll note that I made no earlier mention of braces and bits, hand drills, and other hand-powered drills. The reason is simply the assumption that everyone has at least a lightweight electric drill. Circular saws provide the other essential power tool for carpentry.

To be honest, neither is an absolute essential, but estimates show that carpentry work done with specific portable power tools is on the order of five to seven times faster than using hand tools alone. It is also at least five to seven times easier. I've been watching a neighbor construct a moderate-size shed and I used his photos to illustrate pole and post construction in this book. He has been doing all the nailing by hand. I've been using air-powered framing and finishing nailers and sheathing staplers on my work, and I hope to never do the sort of work being done on that shed. With an air nailer, my neighbor would have been done a week earlier, at least.

Electric Drills. Electric drills offer the widest tool range of all. Points of interest are chuck size, power and comfort in the hand. The pistol grip

electric drill, up through a ½″ chuck, is nearly a standard in the industry. The primary differences in construction are in feel and in what might be classed as point of balance. There are many quality differences as well.

Top-quality drills have more ball bearings, better-fitted cases, longer and heavier power cords that are more easily replaceable, a better-quality chuck, and a more powerful and better-made motor.

You pay for all these features, but if that drill is expected to be in use for heavy work or over a long term, it is worth the extra. For general carpentry and construction work, a ⅜″ chuck is basic, as is variable speed and reversing. Variable speed drills allow you to start drilling without center punching holes (most of the time) to prevent the drill bit's walking off line. Add at least a 3-ampere motor — heavier is better — and you'll do fine. If you wish to do much drilling masonry, get a drill that offers a hammer and drill feature, and use the appropriate masonry hammer drill bits. Cost rises by as much as $50 per tool, but the time and energy savings are considerable.

For driving screws, get a clutched drill. Any variable speed drill does a fair job of driving screws, but a clutched variable speed drill will stop driving the screw before it torques the head off, or before it slides off and mars the work. Specific power drivers for screws are also made.

Cordless electric drills have reached the point where they are almost good enough to replace corded drills in most construction uses. A couple of mine are actually pretty decent hammer drills. Totally avoid the consumer's models, and go for the lower-end professional models. These drills offer the same features as you find in corded drills, with slightly lower capacities in wood, steel and masonry. If you decide to go cordless, get a drill that has a battery pack that charges quickly, preferably in about an hour, and buy a second battery pack. The variety is wide, but for easy use in moderate duty, select a lightweight model in 9.6 volts; for heavier use, jump on a 12-volt version. Price differences aren't bad, but there's no point in slinging around the extra weight of the 12-volt battery if you don't have to.

Circular Saws. Circular saws offer far greater cutting speed than do handsaws, and they are more accurate. A wide variety is on the market, with blade sizes ranging from 4" upward to 16". Industry standard is 7¼", and there is little need for most of us to vary from that.

When circular saw shopping, look for a thick base plate, with some thought given to a drop foot base plate. These are easier to adjust for depth than tilting plates. Also look for an 8' to 10' long cord, a top handle, the 7¼" blade size, and a 10-ampere motor. The lower levels of professional lines are the best place to begin looking.

Many other power and hand tools are available, and you'll form your own list of preferences as you go along. It is quite possible to write an entire book about selection, use and care of carpentry and related tools. For instance, give some thought to getting either a power miter saw or one of the radial arm saws.

Tool Care

Tool care is mostly common sense. Make sure electrical tools have good cords and do not get their plugs mangled. Keep all tools as clean as possible, and lightly oil or otherwise lubricate or protect those that need it. Use tools for the jobs for which they're intended. Screwdrivers are to drive screws, and in a pinch they do well at opening paint cans. They are not pry bars, chisels or levers, and they should not be used as such. (Everyone has used one or more in those ways, afterward wondering why the thing no longer drives screws well.)

In special cases, follow the tool manufacturer's instructions for tool care. In most cases of tool care, keeping the tool clean and dry after use is the main factor in keeping it sharp and working for as long as its quality allows.

Use a round-bristled brush to get off sawdust and other debris, making sure, on electric tools, to get into the vents around the motor. Wipe the tool down with a dry, soft rag. Old, worn-out T-shirts are super for this job. Those tools that tend to collect resin, pitch and gum may need another step or two. For saw blades, a fast wipe with mineral spirits will remove slight traces of gum build-up. Follow this with a coat of very light machine oil. For blades that get heavy use, and thus build up heavy coatings of gums, more severe measures are needed. There are commercial gum dissolvers that work well with circular saw and other blades, but probably the best, and cheapest, gum remover is oven cleaner. The heavy lye base eats gum off rapidly, and a wipe with a damp sponge gets rid of the residue. Keep the sponge well rinsed in tepid water.

Once the last bits of gum and cleaner are off, use a good coating of machine oil to protect the blade from rust, again locating an old T-shirt to dry the blade thoroughly. Water does not harm metal, unless it is left to stand and start a rust cycle that soon ruins any tool.

You can clean any tool with water and dishwashing detergent when grease and other dirt builds up beyond the point where it can be easily removed by wiping with a dry cloth. Use soft cloths, rinse well, and make sure that no electric motor windings get wet. Dry thoroughly, and then liberally coat any exposed steel or iron parts with light machine oil.

The primary objection to oiling any saw blade, plane iron or similar wood-cutting device, is the effect the lubricant has on wood finishes. Wood finishes don't stick over oily substances. This doesn't much matter if you are cutting framing stock, but on siding and in other areas where finishes will be applied, you want to make 2' or longer cleaning cuts with any blade before applying the blade to good wood.

Tool Safety

Tool safety is also a matter of common sense, but it requires some knowledge. Make sure you have a clear cutting line and that tool cords will not snag as you cut. Snags usually just pull the cut off line, wasting material, but at others times can cause a tool to be yanked loose from the cut and the hand, at which time the tool is dangerous.

Wear eye protection, whether safety glasses, goggles or a face shield. If goggles and glasses steam up on you often, try a face shield. If steaming is still a problem with a face shield, you can cut three or four ³⁄₁₆" slots, about 1½" long, in front of the mouth and nose areas of the shield.

Keep the area around your feet clear. Make sure extra tools, lumber and cut-offs, plus general scraps and junk, do not trip or otherwise interfere with your free movement and work.

Follow the manufacturer's specific safety instructions for any tool. Check for the direction of force with all tools, and specifically check for the direction of kickback that is apt to occur with power tools. Circular saws and table saws obviously differ, but both kick back strongly. A jammed circular saw will kick itself back toward the worker, so make sure the lower blade guard drops into place freely. It also helps to stand slightly to one side when working with circular saws. Table saws kick back the material because the tool, in most cases, is too heavy to move (this may not hold true with some of the newer lightweight benchtop saws). Make sure guards are in place and correctly adjusted, and keep your body out of line of possible kickback, while making sure no one else walks through the kickback path during saw use.

Always think before, and while, you work. Keep safe tool use foremost in your mind.

FOUNDATIONS

The foundation type for any free-standing woodworking shop will depend on several factors: the site, the size of the shop to be built, your desires and skills, and the thickness of your wallet. If you can afford anything you want, the shop layout and tool selection planning sections of this book are probably all you need to read. If you must do most or all of the work, you'll want more detail on techniques of construction. There are

This pole building frame has 6″ × 6″ corner posts, buried 3′ in heavy clay soil. Intermediate 4″ × 4″ posts are also buried 3′. Remember to check your local code for frost line information.

a slew of construction methods that are suitable for shop construction, ranging from the least costly—usually pole building—to standard platform framing.

Pole Building

Pole building works as its own foundation but doesn't have a widely accepted method of planting the poles. Most published information is on methods used in hard freeze areas of what might well be classed as the northern United States. In those sites, pole selection, hole digging and backfilling methods are exceptionally complex, as they are in areas with sandy soils. I would avoid pole building in such areas, except for the simplest sheds, because by the time you get a backhoe in to dig the holes and then backfill with soil cement, the cost approaches that of pouring a 4″ thick concrete pad.

For more reasonable areas, where the frost line is less than 30″, the soil requires nothing but a dirt backfill on 48″ or shallower holes. This is for poles that are above around less than 12′. Pole construction is cheap and fast. Rent or borrow a tractor with power take-off and a 12″ or larger auger posthole digger. Pop in your holes, and clean the bottoms. Insert poles, and plumb—round poles are plumbed on only one side, but square poles are plumbed on all sides.

Next, brace and backfill. If you're on reasonably level ground and are pouring a concrete floor, it's probably simplest to use two 2″ × 6″ base braces on the exterior of the poles as general guides and forms for the floor. Use bolts or lag screws to attach the top 2″ × 6″ to the posts (a minimum of ⅜″ × 4″ lag screws, one per post, plus at least two 3½″ [16d] nails). Attach the bottom board to the posts with three 16d nails per post. A ⁵⁄₁₆″ × 3½″ lag screw plus two nails is even better. If you cover the boards with siding, the lag screw heads should be set into a hole to allow the siding to lie flat. Drill such holes—counterbores—in a large enough diameter to accept a flat washer under the bolt or screw head. Poles and these lower boards must all be of pressure-treated, or creosoted, wood. My neighbor is currently building a shed of some size, using what I would class as posts instead of poles. The shed will have corners of 6″ × 6″ pressure-treated, dried lumber, with 4″ × 4″ intermediate posts. The other construction is standard pole building, but such use, though more costly, makes nailing easier.

Use a level on the top edge of the bottom board to set your line, and drive the nails first. Then drill and bolt, or screw, the boards in place.

Once the boards are in place, lay

2″ × 4″ nailers with a 2″ × 6″ lower brace.

in 6″ of clean gravel, and cover that with 10-mil polyethylene sheeting, overlapped at least 18″. Be careful not to rip the sheeting. Lay in reinforcement netting for the concrete, and have the floor poured and smoothed. It is not my object here to explain the dynamics of pouring and smoothing a concrete floor, as that's been done well by others. Unless you've got considerable experience with concrete, I suggest you quit at the pouring stage, and have someone else do

the finish work. Finish takes special tools and a lot of skill, and it is something you can usually get done for a specified price per square foot.

As you'll have noted, I'm not a lover of concrete floors in shops for several reasons. Their lack of give can make your legs awfully tired when you work a lot of hours on a project. The first time you drop a new $35 or $40 chisel point-first onto concrete, you'll understand my other objection. Concrete can and should be

Side bracing and 2″ × 4″ rafters for a shed roof finish the exterior framing of this pole structure.

painted to prevent its dusting. It may also be covered with sheet or tile vinyl. Neither replaces a good wood floor, but both are better than bare concrete.

Framing for Pole Construction.
Pole construction requires a different type of framing, in general. Instead of vertical studs, you place horizontal nailers. The nailers can be of almost any junk wood, as long as they provide a solid surface for nailing.

In most of the examples I can provide, nailers are of green or almost green, rough-sawn wood direct from the sawmill. These are nailed on the outside of the poles, and the siding is nailed to them. The work goes quickly. Poles are normally placed on

8′ centers. You can overlap with boards, using 16′ long boards to form a unit of three posts. It's very easy to keep from breaking joints on the same post, though the nailers are not really needed as structural members. Such methods do tend to stiffen the nailers. Use a minimum 3½″ nail here, three per post, and a dab of waterproof construction adhesive. Set nailers on 24″ vertical centers.

Roof framing is the same as for any kinds of structure, with the poles being topped with 2″ × 6″ lumber and the rafters set onto the top edges of that lumber. You may be able to use shed roof styles if the span isn't too great.

Platform Framing
Platform framing is the method of choice for many buildings. Most residences in this country are built this way, and so are many middle-size outbuildings. The method allows great flexibility and is fairly low in cost. And a wide variety of foundation types may be used.

Poured concrete floors work well but are built differently for platform-framed structures than for pole buildings. You lay out the building size, then set forms for the floor. The procedure in laying gravel, sheeting, reinforcement wire and pouring cement is the same, but you set anchor bolts around the perimeter, spaced no more than 8′ apart, and tilt your

Tilting up a framed platform wall.

A poured concrete platform.

walls onto those bolts. Then you run down a nut over a washer to keep the walls from blowing off in storms. Walls are constructed on the poured floor and tilted into place, where they are plumbed and braced until joining walls are attached.

Crawl Spaces and Piers. Crawl spaces also work well with platform framing. A footing set below the frost line is dug and poured, then concrete block is laid on the footing. Codes will require a minimum two block height above grade. You insert at least two screened ventilators in the crawl space walls so that moisture doesn't build too high and cause rot.

Piers are placed on footings, again at the proper depth for your weather, and can be erected in a little less time than crawl space foundations. Layout tends to be slightly more complex, because you need two rows up the outside edges of the structure and a central row as well. But once laid out, the holes are more quickly dug than are full footing trenches, and laying four block per pier is faster than

This concrete floor has poured concrete footings and foundation, fairly unusual construction for a shop.

laying a two block high foundation around the full perimeter. In some areas, you may also elect to use posts as piers, with a precast concrete collar and soil cement as a backfill.

From this point, I will describe the construction of a platform-framed building, 24′ × 40′, on a crawl space

foundation, with some notes to cover other situations. The idea is to keep costs as low as possible, so we're looking at several options for roofing and siding, some of which are more economical in installation than in actual cost. Some forms of metal roof, for example, are almost as costly

Concrete block is more usual in shop foundation walls.

to install as are shingles, but they go on so quickly they save labor time. If you do your own labor, the savings are small. But if you can find a person who has overbought some form of roofing material, whether metal or asphalt/fiberglass shingle, you can save lots of money. Don't check only dealers for this kind of savings. Talk to local builders and see who might have misjudged a job or lost a job after buying materials.

SITE SELECTION AND BUILDING LAYOUT

You want to build a shop. And you've got some space in your yard. Sticking the shop in that space makes sense, so you locate a corner and go.

If you do, I hope you're a lucky type, because a number of considera-tions need a bit of earlier thought. First is the location of the new struc-ture in relation to existing structures, walkways, power lines, septic fields and tanks, sewage lines, water lines, wells, driveways, trees, bushes, vari-ous garden spaces, springs, and power company access lines, as well as the general lay of the ground. Al-ways check local codes before getting started with any structure, and pay attention to what they say about set-backs. Some codes specify 10', and some are 15'.

On my property, which amounts to almost two acres and has plenty of space behind the house, we've got fruit trees spaced along one area that must have sunlight. And we've got young shade trees in other areas, a patio in another, and a deck off the back of the house. We also have to extend both the deck and the house in the near future. And our septic field takes almost one entire side of the lot near the house. Then the back corner of the lot is too steep to ac-commodate a building, and it faces forward onto a spring that flows year-round in an area that my wife is slowly turning into a rock garden al-most ⅛ acre in size.

Then the power pole is on the op-posite corner of the lot from where I'd really like to place the shop, so I have to think of costs of adding poles. The local power company doesn't like to use consumer-installed poles, and I need a separate service to the shop, as most of you will if you elect to go with a large enough shop to require a freestand-ing building. See chapter four, on electrical service, for details of those needs.

My assumption for my shop is a portable potty and a garden hose for any water needs, but some of you may wish to go further. I'll go as far as running a frost-free standing tap to within about 10' of the new building. It makes clean-up simpler to have at least some access to water. I'd like to put in a full set, hot and cold, and drains, but the price goes up accord-ingly, so that's out of the question.

All this and much else must be taken into consideration.

My final site is almost level, a fac-tor that saves a great deal of money when it comes time to pour a founda-tion or floor. There is sufficient space for a building of at least 32' × 52', and my planned structure will be 24' × 40', though it may reach to 44' if finances permit. That still allows space for the outside staircase to the upper floor, where I plan to put an office.

So site your shop with reference to all the variables above, and any others that might fit your locale and situation.

Setting Corners and Batter Boards

Determine where one corner of the building will lie, and drive a peg at that spot. Now, make up some batter boards. These consist of eight pieces of 1" × 4" or 1" × 5" material, each nailed to 2" × 4"s. The first batter board is notched in the center to ac-cept a cord, and the 2" × 4"s have points cut on their ends. Your 2" × 4" length will vary depending on the site. Level sites require 2" × 4"s only 18" or so long, while you may run into a need for some as long as 6' in hilly terrain. The usual type of batter board uses three 2" × 4"s and two boards, nailed as shown in the draw-ings. Each batter board is saw-kerfed (slotted) when the spot for the mason's cord is determined. Drive the first batter board assembly in place about 4' behind and outside the peg marking one corner, but roughly aligned so the cord notch will let you carry mason's cord directly over the peg and on to the next corner. Drive a second set of batter boards about 4' past the spot for the next corner, parallel to and facing the first set, if you're using the two-piece units.

When all four corners are in place and batter boards are set level, run the mason's cord as shown in the drawings, and settle it around until you've got square corners. There are two ways to make sure your corners are square. Use the 3-4-5 (or $9' \times 12' \times 15'$, as in the drawing) triangle method to determine square, or measure the diagonals and make

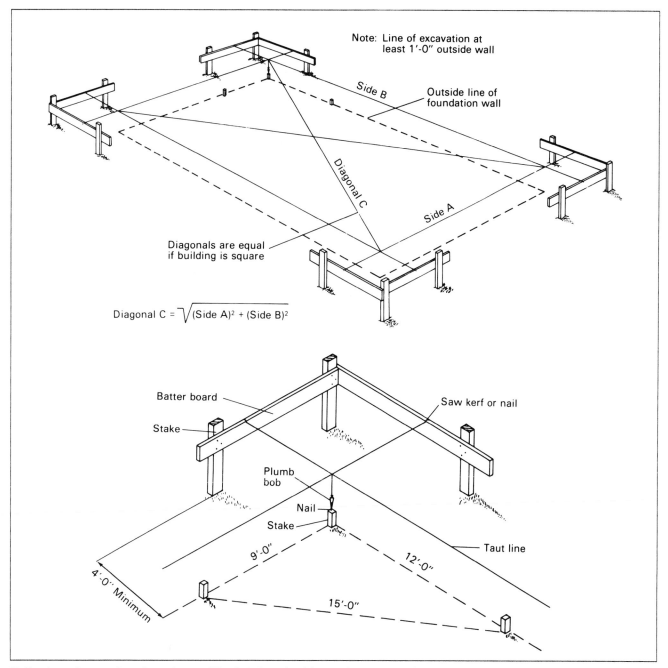

Batter boards are placed as shown. The 3-4-5 method is used to square the corners. Once the corners are squared, check to make sure diagonal measurements are equal. That's the final test of squareness.

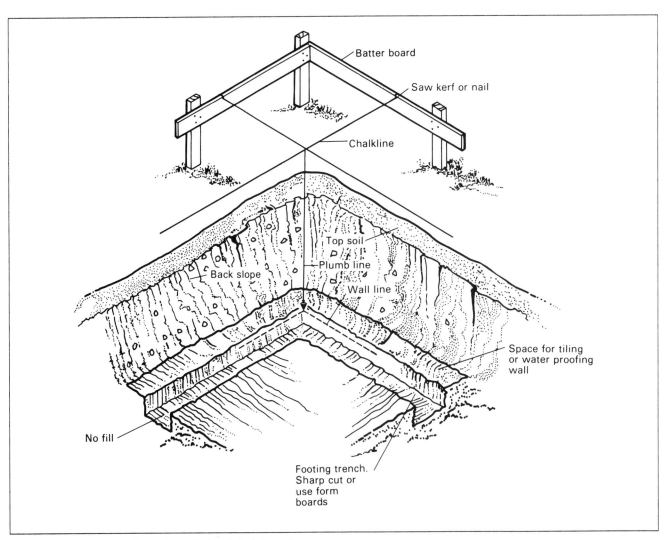

Excavating with batter boards and plumb bob is not easy.

sure they are exactly equal. I suggest you use both methods, one as a check on the other. Unless you erect moderate-size structures frequently, you'll find you waste far less time over finicky measurements than you do if you goof and waste materials.

Once the cords are set, kerf the batter boards that aren't already notched, and set the cords in, pulling them tight. Using a very light plumb bob, drop your measurement to the ground, centering it on a stake with a nail in it.

There are some major variations in construction methods from this point on: For pole construction, I like to drive a small (1″ × 1″) stake dead in the center of each pole location. For poured concrete floors and crawl spaces, the excavation line is about 1′ outside the line formed by the mason's cord. For pier foundations, you work a sort of half-and-half setup, with exterior lines of pier footings set 1′ to the outside of the line, plus about double whatever extra width you need to match your blocks. With standard 8″ blocks, which are 16″ (nominally) long, you

need a 32″ wide footing. If you can locate them readily, go with 6″ blocks, and you get a 2′ wide footer. Footings are always at least twice as wide as the wall or other object being placed on them. For a 32″ wide footing, go 24″ outside the mason's cord. For a 24″ footing, go 16″. These are minimal settings, as a standard crawl space wall footing is 16″ wide. The block that rests on that footing is nominally 8″ wide.

Once the foundation is in, floor-framing starts.

The cord holder helps you keep a straight course as you lay block.

A level makes sure all is right before the cord holder is used.

Corners rise as shown. Note that two cord holders are used, one in each direction from the corner.

CHAPTER 8

FRAMING AND SHEATHING THE FREESTANDING SHOP

F raming and covering a shop building gets you to where you itch to work on projects of somewhat smaller size. And this chapter should let you get to the point of moving in and setting up your tools.

FRAMING FLOORS

Floor-framing is a fairly simple matter for shop structures, because most are done without stairwells, interior partition plans and similar fancy stuff. Depending on the width of the shop, you need joists of a particular size, as indicated by the charts. In most cases, 2″ × 8″ or 2″ × 10″ joists more than suffice. Maximum spans for each on 24″ centers goes about 10′ to 14′ from the center of one member, in this case a joist, to the center of another. If you use Southern pine, those figures can be stretched a bit, but they should be fudged if you use white pine.

Sills are the base for the entire

This pressure-treated sill is on a concrete floor, so no termite shield is required. The sill was nailed to three day old concrete, a very easy job. Concrete continues to harden as it ages but is fairly soft at the three day stage, so nailing is as easy as it gets.

floor frame. They come in several different types, yet all are constructed of 2″ dimension lumber. A flat 2″ × 6″ or 2″ × 8″ sill board bolted to the foundation is used for crawl space walls. The sill in a concrete floored

place is nothing more than the sole plate of the stud wall unit, bolted to the foundation. The poured concrete slab has J-bolts that are attached to the sill at 2′ intervals. Check local codes both for intervals and anchor bolt sizes and types. Sills on pier foundations are simply the outsides of the unit, with boards set horizontally at right angles to the floor joists. There may be one, two or three sill boards, depending on size requirements. For piers, the joists are doubled when piers are 8′ on one center, and a center beam of three boards is used to double the span using a center row of piers. These may be 12′ on center.

In pier or platform post construction, joists are either set upon or hung from the sills. Sills need to be protected from termites; they are best made of pressure-treated wood, even though they'll be protected from weather and won't contact the ground. A .40 pounds per cubic foot protection is enough. A termite shield is also helpful. Termite shields are of metal, usually aluminum, and are formed at least 3″ wider than the sill, with 1½″ of the outside edge, turned about 10 degrees downward. If the shield is on a pier or crawl space, the 1½″ inside edge should also be turned 10 degrees downward. Termites can't tunnel over this, and any that somehow manage to reach the sill are defeated by the pressure-treated lumber.

From here, frame the floor using a three-member center beam, if needed. Remember, spans of more than 14′ require the center beam. Set the sills and center beam using joist hangers.

To place joists, start from the center of both the beam and the outside sill and measure the *outside* distances. Check width of actual joists. Nominal 2″ lumber yard materials will be a standard 1½″ thick, but sawmill lumber may vary from 2″ to 2½″ thick. Use half that distance to mark

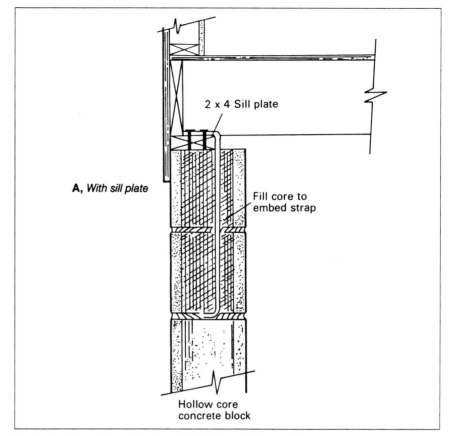

Typical sill configuration for a block foundation wall.

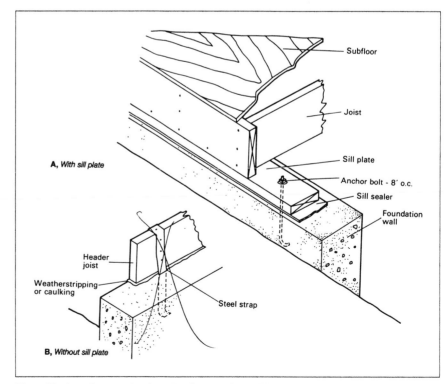

The sill plate is attached to the foundation with anchor bolts that are buried into the foundation while the cement is still wet.

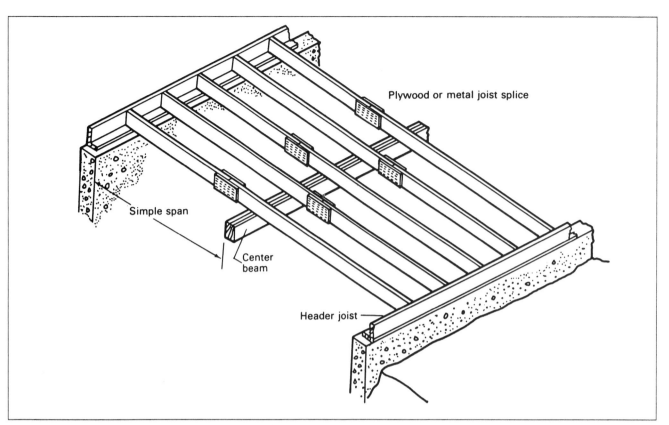

Joists form the webbing that supports the floor. Splicing is shown as allowing use of shorter lengths of material, but the job is better if equal lengths are used and butted over the beam — or set alongside each other.

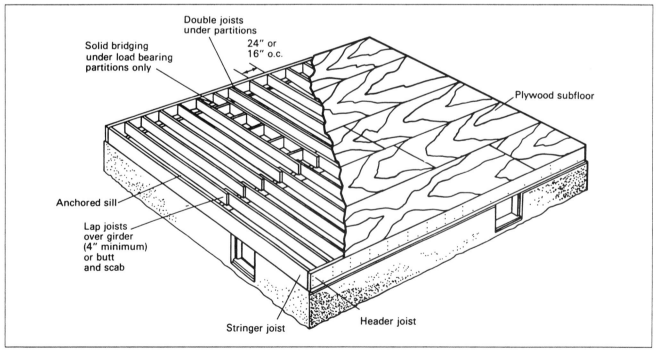

Note overlapping joists and solid bridging in this floor framing layout. This drawing has almost all the detail needed to get a floor framed and a subfloor in place.

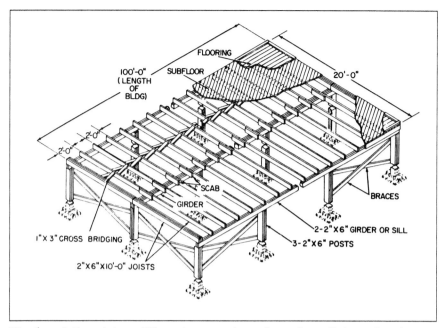

Pier foundations take a different approach as shown here. It doesn't make any difference what material is used for the piers.

Mark for stud placement. The X is always on the side covered by the stud.

one edge of each joist position, and use a square to drop the line down the face of both beams and joists.

Use joist hangers or toenail joists in place at 16″ or 24″ intervals. In most cases, and certainly with more standard strength and size lumber, you'll want to go with 2″ × 10″s on that span. Use 16d or 20d nails, three per joint. A dab of construction adhesive is a good thing, too, but don't make mistakes. Once this stuff sets up, it doesn't let go.

Placing Flooring

Here is one of the best methods I've seen of reducing flooring costs and getting a sturdy, two-layer floor similar to those used in wood-floored residences. This is rough-cut 1″ sawmill yellow pine for a subfloor, placed at a 45-degree angle to the joists and nailed with 2¾″ (8d) nails. This is not unusual, though plywood has become the subfloor of choice in residences. Use a dab or two of construction cement on each joist as the subfloor passes over.

Next, place a final floor of ⅝″ tongue-and-groove sanded plywood, using 2¼″ (6d) nails, 6″ apart on the edges and 8″ apart on inner nailing lines. Then coat the plywood with four layers of polyurethane. The resulting floor is sturdy, squeak-free, and easy to clean and maintain, while being as easy as possible on the legs and feet. Frame out the walls and tilt them into place.

Always keep hands well free of air nailer tip. These nailers are an easy way to frame.

FRAMING WALLS

Standard 24″ on center (*outside*) framing is best for walls in shops. You may, if you wish, use the slightly more sturdy 16″ outside spacing, but for all practical purposes, the 24″ outside is a good standard. The wider distance is almost universally accepted now, but, again, it's wise to check local codes.

Note details of framing for windows and doors in the drawings. These details are easily taken care of in planning stages and in framing the units on the floor. Careful layout and cutting is essential to easy final assembly. Usually, door and window rough openings are made to within about ½″ to 1″ of the actual size of the door frame to be set into the opening. For headers with spans less than 4′, use 2″ × 6″s. For larger spans, use 2″ × 8″s, doubled, and with ½″ plywood separators to get it out to size with the rest of the framing. If you use rough-cut lumber for framing, change the spacer thickness appropriately. You need separators only at about 1½″ around the perimeters of the headers. Window sills are placed and supported with cripple studs, which are short studs, cut to fit a particular need such as this, at ends and center. Walls are framed with a doubled top plate that is left an appropriate distance from each end, where an added piece ties the adjoining wall in tightly.

Tilt the completed, braced wall into place, and secure it with braces to the floor. You will need helpers here, unless the wall is exceptionally light and short. I've done and seen large walls with one person doing all the work, but it is no fun, and it can prove dangerous. Either nail the wall to the subfloor or bolt it to the an-

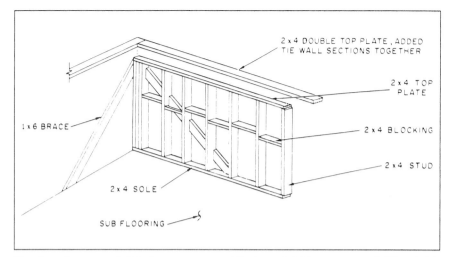

Bracing shown on left is temporary, and that on right is permanent. The right hand type isn't needed if plywood, oriented strand board or waferboard is used on the corners.

Two people make the job go faster and aid accuracy.

When both sides of corners are framed and covered with oriented strand board or waferboard, you don't need inlet bracing, but temporary bracing remains until roof sheathing is on.

The framed wall is tipped into place. Here the studs are to be toenailed to the already placed sole plate. Other builders prefer to make the entire wall frame and nail it to the floor as it is stood in place.

The wall is in place and ready to be nailed there.

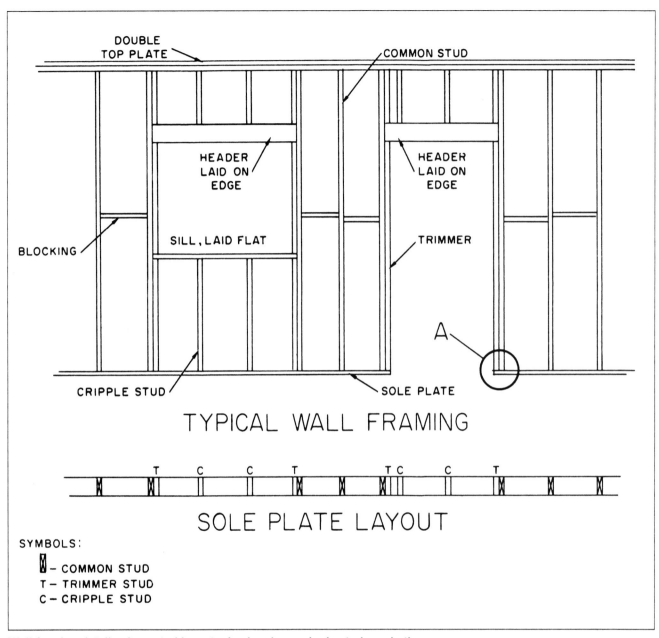

DOUBLE
TOP PLATE

COMMON STUD

HEADER
LAID ON
EDGE

HEADER
LAID ON
EDGE

BLOCKING

SILL, LAID FLAT

TRIMMER

A

CRIPPLE STUD

SOLE PLATE

TYPICAL WALL FRAMING

T   C   C   T   T C   C   T

SOLE PLATE LAYOUT

SYMBOLS:

▓ – COMMON STUD
T – TRIMMER STUD
C – CRIPPLE STUD

Wall-framing details show stud layout, plus headers, cripple studs and other parts.

chor bolts in the concrete floor, through the holes in the sole plate. The wall must be accurately plumbed before being finally tied down tightly and must be well braced before you go on to framing and placing adjoining walls. Usually, bracing is done with 2″ × 4″ material, to the ground or to the foundation wall, depending on site needs.

With the framed walls in place, it's time to frame the roof. In most manuals, you'll find wall sheathing and such covered at this point. That's all well and good, but if you live in an area where it rains with some frequency, it's best to tie in the roof system. This will not only protect the framing underneath, but will also strengthen the overall structure.

ROOF FRAMING

The easiest, most sensible way to frame a roof is to use trusses, whether you're framing a cement block structure, a platform framed building or a pole structure. You save time and energy by using trusses, though you do lose some storage space in the rafter area, and the cost is about double that of stick-built rafters and ceiling

This shot shows the header, lower sill and cripple studs. Header and sills *must* rest on cripple studs on both sides. Cripple studs are nothing more than studs that have been cut shorter than full-length.

joists. Still, it is faster, cleaner and usually stronger to go with trusses, and unless you've put up an immense building, the cost isn't that bad. It doesn't matter what kind of roof you will install. Trusses are, like rafters, adaptable to most all you're apt to use. There's another advantage to using trusses: The entire span distance is free span. Otherwise known as wide open, *free span* means you will have 24′ of open width for 24′ of span, minus the distances of the

framing for walls and wallboard.

If you use a short-run shed roof, as you see in our pole building example, forget trusses. That span is only about a dozen feet, and it is done with 2″ × 6″s. Otherwise, rafters are too much work.

Trusses require at least two people on site, and a crane is a help with larger spans. For trusses spanning up to 28′, three people to help are usually enough.

All roofing work requires great

Truss types: A is a W truss; B is a King post truss; C is a scissors truss. The W truss is the most common in the Southeast.

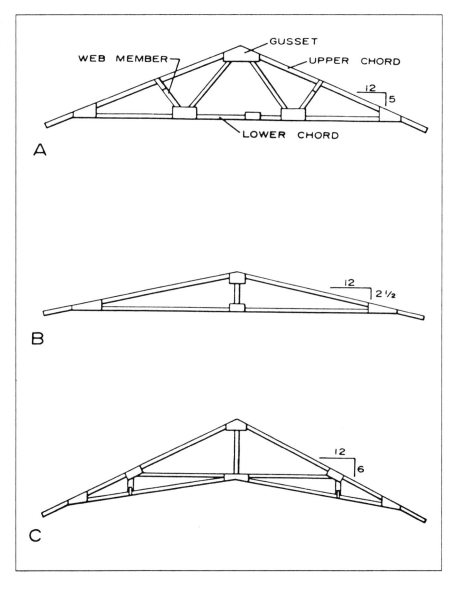

care. You're off the ground, so make sure you're securely seated or have good footing at all times. I'm terrified of heights, so I am extremely careful when working on a roof system.

Trusses are spaced 24″ outside and are nailed into the top plate. Toenail the trusses to the top plate with 16d nails if no anchors are used. Use the correct nails for the type if anchors are used.

ROOFING

Roofing is a far more complex subject than this treatment will consider. In this book, we will quickly look at only two methods of roofing.

Roof sheathing goes on first. It is used on 24″ on-center construction, with 7/16″ oriented strand board, waferboard or CDX plywood if you're placing shingles. You use recommended nailing patterns, usually with 6d nails at 6″ intervals on the outside edges of the sheets, and at 8″ intervals up the inside nailing lines of the sheets. Do not ever break two butting sheets of plywood on the same joist. To achieve this, simply start the first row with a full sheet of plywood, and the second with a half sheet.

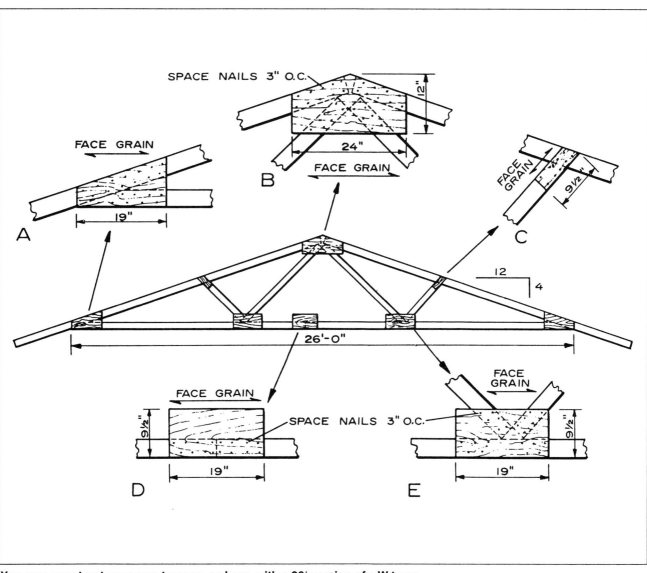

You may construct your own trusses, as here, with a 26′ version of a W truss. Commercial metal plates may also be used. The angled wood plates here, of ½″ or ⅝″ CDX plywood, may be pad cut on a band saw, a dozen or more at a time. Use construction adhesive and 6d nails to fasten.

If you're placing metal roofing, use nailers at 24″ intervals, making those nailers cross the rafters at right angles. Do not break nailers on the same joist if they're directly in line up the roof. No sheathing is used.

The nails used will vary in length depending on the thickness of the nailers. Though our shed uses 2″ × 4″ stock, which requires at least a 3½″ (16d) nail, much work is done with 1″ stock that takes a 3″ (9d) nail.

Underlayment

You also need what manufacturers call "asphalt felt saturated underlayment," commonly known as tar paper. Add enough drip edging to cover the eaves and the gable ends. Start the entire job by applying the drip edging along the eaves, nailing, with flathead galvanized roofing nails, every 10″. Then lay the tar paper, overlapping at least 6″ over each preceding course. If you run out of a roll

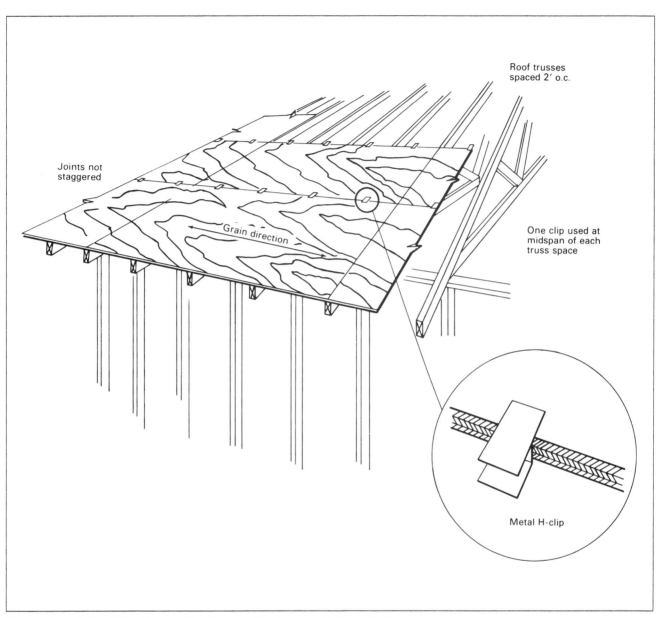

Roof trusses
spaced 2' o.c.

Joints not
staggered

Grain direction

One clip used at
midspan of each
truss space

Metal H-clip

Plywood roof sheathing is normally placed with staggered joints — that is, no two sheets will line up directly above each other with a break on the same rafter — but the in-line use is considered acceptable *if* an H clip is used at the midpoint between every truss.

and start another in midcourse, overlap at least 6″ and make sure the lap is 6′ from any end or obstruction. If you've added a chimney, carry the underlayment 4″ up the vertical side of that chimney.

Underlayment is used to protect the roof deck until shingles are down, and it also serves to protect the roof deck if shingles are later damaged.

Do not use impermeable materials such as polyethylene sheeting for this job, as water must be able to slowly percolate out of under-roof areas.

The last of the drip edging goes on the gable ends, over the tar paper.

Flashing

We're not looking at valley flashing in this book because the roof isn't

supposed to cover a complex enough building to require valleys. For flashing around chimneys, extend apron flashing across the front and rear of the chimney, and use step flashing on the sides. Bend all to a right angle, with half running up the vertical and half on the horizontal, but with the step flashing designed to allow steps up the roof. The top of the flashing

My neighbor brought his 2″ × 4″ nailers up and onto the rafters a few days later. The roof is extra strong for walking on, but it requires a longer nail and is more expensive overall.

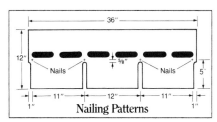

The nailing pattern for a three-tab asphalt shingle.

Georgia-Pacific Corporation.

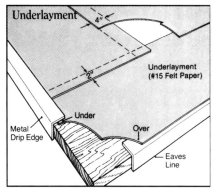

Eave drip guard placement. Note the arrangement of the underlayment over the drip guards, too.

Georgia-Pacific Corporation.

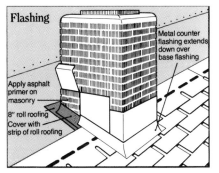

Flashing for a chimney is simple to do but is critical to a tight roof.

Georgia-Pacific Corporation.

should be placed in mortar joints or cut lines and covered moderately with top-quality asphalt coating. The bottom of the apron flashing goes over the shingle below it, but the step flashing goes under the shingles. Each succeeding step flashing piece goes over the one below it and feeds onto the apron.

With flashing on or ready, lay out chalk lines on the tar-papered roof.

Do not depend on the lines printed on the paper. It may not be on exactly straight, and the lines are not close enough together. Lay out chalk lines the depth of the shingles, minus ⅜″, up the roof for the first one. Then mark the depth of the shingles from the top edge of the first course, and each succeeding course, on up the roof. Usually, shingles are 12″ deep, but that varies, so you should check

111

and lay your lines accordingly.

For shingled roofs, first measure the roof to see how much material you need. Shingles are sold in bundles, three bundles to the square, which is a unit that gives you 100 square feet of exposed shingle roofing. Prices vary all over the place depending on durability, style, color and other factors. I suggest you look for a moderately priced twenty-five year fiberglass/asphalt shingle in a simple pattern. In most areas of the United States, you want a light color to reflect heat away during summer months. In the North and in Canada, you want a darker color to absorb heat during the longer cold months.

Laying Shingles

Shingles are laid in a specific manner, but often manufacturers include nailing patterns and layout patterns that differ somewhat. *Always* begin by reversing a first course of shingles, laying them with tabs toward the ridge line, and nailing in the tabs. Allow about ⅜″ overhang. Next, the first real course goes over this reversed line and gets the same amount of overhang. Start the course with a full shingle. Start the second course with a half shingle, and the third course with a third of a shingle, after which you repeat the full shingle, and go on up until you reach the ridge line. Repeat the process on the second side.

At the ridge line, I recommend that you use a commercial ridge vent, or you can cut shingles between tabs and use them to form the ridge. This is called a Boston ridge, and it works well.

Metal Roofing

Metal roofing goes on over nailers spaced 2′ apart up the rafters. The

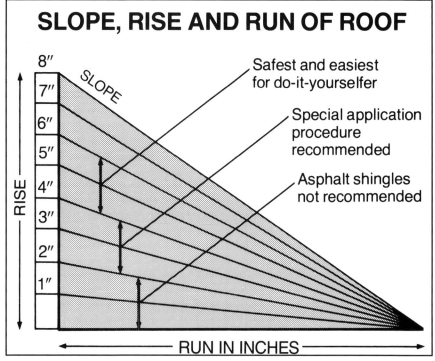

The chart shows the slope where asphalt shingles are best — and the easiest for do-it-yourselfers to work. Too low a slope means the roof will leak, and too great a slope needs to be left to professionals.

Georgia-Pacific Corporation.

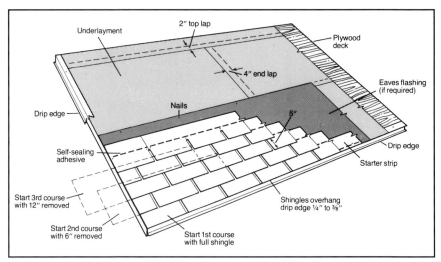

This pattern for laying shingles is for plywood decking; it's called the 6″ method.

Georgia-Pacific Corporation.

roofing is available in varying widths, but usually it's got a 2′ or 3′ exposure for width, and lengths may range from 6′ to 16′. It is not essential to have edges meet at rafters, but a good nailing pattern must be established. I'm more comfortable if metal roofing is screwed down instead of nailed. Clutched cordless drills make this a simple job, and you need only

Note the safety goggles, safety rope and sneakers on the worker.

Georgia-Pacific Corporation.

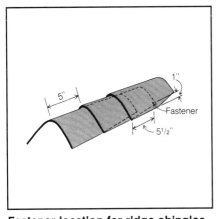

Fastener location for ridge shingles.

Asphalt Roofing Manufacturers' Association.

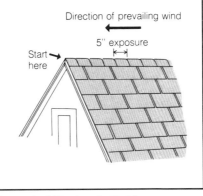

Layout of Boston butt ridge.

Asphalt Roofing Manufacturers' Association.

use the length and style of screw recommended by the roof manufacturer. Usually, these screws will be 1½" or 2" long, and they may have little rubber washers to serve as gaskets.

Aluminum roofing is easier to deal with than galvanized, but galvanized tends to be considerably cheaper. It pays to consider different materials, methods and timing. Also, check the newspaper for sale ads, among other sources.

Sheet roofing goes on quickly, though handling 12′ × 3′ sheets only makes sense when there are two people on the job.

There are disadvantages to sheet metal roofing, too, and they must be considered. The stuff provides no R value at all. Both heat and cold are immediately, or nearly so, passed on through. Thus, you roast in summer and shiver in winter, and a wood stove or other heater doesn't help a lot unless it's kept well stoked. Air conditioning for a hobby wood shop is not practical, but big fans are. You'll need lots of windows and huge fans with a tin roof.

Another solution, which I recommend, is that you insulate, using a minimum of 3½" of fiberglass insulation. If you place a ceiling on the trusses, then you might want to lay in 6" to 12" of insulation — this is an idea that works well with any style of roof but is nearly essential with metal roofing. Insulation is often on sale but is seldom sold as overstock, so wild price reductions aren't frequent, though it pays to check around. I've found as much as five bucks a bundle (about 50 square feet) difference in price locally for the same materials.

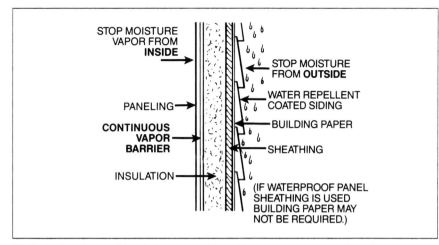

Wall design for residential construction. You may or may not insulate your shop walls, but vapor barriers are essential if the wall is closed. Use building paper for exterior sheathing.

Georgia-Pacific Corporation.

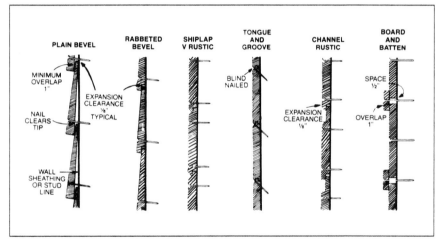

Nailing patterns for siding of different types. You probably will use plain beveled, flat lap, or board and batten siding. Board on board is like board and batten, but it uses wider stock.

Georgia-Pacific Corporation.

WALL SHEATHING AND FINISH

Once the roof is under cover, sheathed and covered with tar paper, or fully covered with a tin roof, consider enclosing the sides of the shop. We've covered all the planning needs for doors and windows, and you know my view on standard windows in the shop: great for ventilation, but lousy for light.

Side wall sheathing is carried out to the window and door frame edges and right to the corners. Use either plywood, sheathing insulation board that is reasonably cheap, waferboard, oriented strand board, or 1″ × 6″ pine or poplar rough or planed sheathing board. The latter two are probably the cheapest, but they take the longest and are the most difficult to install, as they must be installed at a diagonal (45 degrees) to the studs. It's necessary in other cases to let in

bracing for flat, 90-degree-to-the-stud installations. Let-in bracing is cut into the studs at a 45-degree angle. This is very time consuming. Either run the board sheathing at an angle, buy commercial metal bracing, or use plywood or engineered board.

For plywood and similar materials, use the plywood oriented strand board or waferboard on the corners covering three studs. With 24″ outside framing, cover four studs in 16″ outside work. The material is applied vertically and is nailed at 6″ intervals along the outsides and 8″ intervals on the inside nailing line or lines. Again, construction adhesive helps add structural rigidity.

With the corners braced with the plywood, you can then use homosote or other insulating board to finish out the sheathing. That's cheaper and more effective in the long run.

In pole construction, wall-framing is done inside the poles, and there is no need for headers over doors and windows. Simply use cripple studs from a horizontal member to the top plate. The framing doesn't support any of the building's weight. I'd suggest doing the framing on the inside edge of the poles, setting a plumb line there for any later interior finish walls.

Siding goes on over the sheathing, where sheathing is used. Start by placing molding boards on building corners and around doors and windows. Siding, whether vertical or horizontal, butts on these boards. Seal the resulting small cracks with caulking compound.

SIDING MATERIAL AND APPLICATION

You may use plywood siding, board siding, or any of the other available

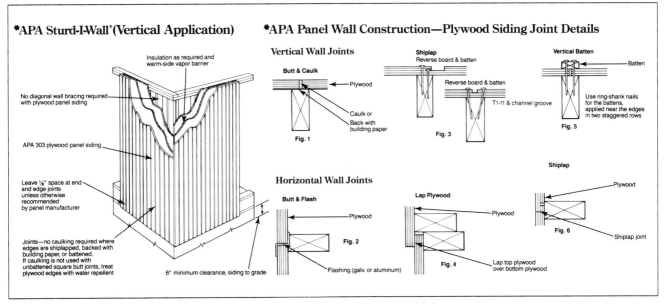

*APA Sturd-I-Wall® (Vertical Application)

*APA Panel Wall Construction—Plywood Siding Joint Details

American Plywood Association vertical plywood installation has some special needs, as shown, depending on the siding type used.

materials. One company, Georgia-Pacific, emphasizes vinyl, hardboard, and a new type of plywood that looks like beaded tongue-and-groove material.

You may also, as Bobby Weaver and I did, choose to use rough-cut lumber direct from the sawmill, set horizontally as clapboards. True clapboards are cut in a taper across the width, but rough-cut material goes up nicely as clapboard without the fanciness. I used a sheathing stapler and 2″ coated staples and will let the siding remain for about a year before coming back with any kind of finish coat. At that time, I'll use a dense stain instead of paint. There is less pigment, and thus a more permeable final coat, with opaque exterior stains. The greater permeability of the final coat means there's less chance of blistering later on.

Vertical board and horizontal board siding must have sheathing underneath for stability. Plywood adds an amazing amount of rigidity that 6″ boards do not.

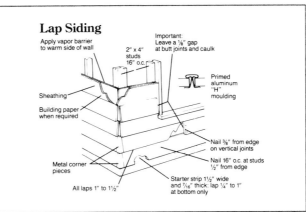

Lap siding starts with installation of the corners, both inside and outside, and any needed door and window molding. Leave ⅛″ gaps for caulking.

Georgia-Pacific Corporation.

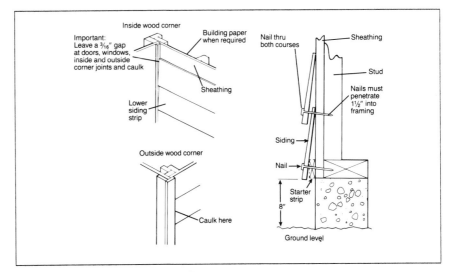

Detail of corner boards and nailing.

Georgia-Pacific Corporation.

For either type of siding, snap a level line around the base of the woodshop sheathing, so that you have a starting point. You should have already nailed all corner molding and window and door molding in place. Corner molding is usually made 1" to 4" longer than the siding is low.

Start horizontal board siding in one corner, at the bottom, and nail at the top and halfway down the middle of the course. I use a sheathing stapler with 2" staples, and I find it saves a lot of hassle trying to hold a strip of siding in place while I drive that first nail. Wham, and the first staple is in with just a squeeze of the trigger. These can be rented at most tool rental shops.

Corner waferboard serves as corner bracing. Both sides of the corner must be covered, and the nailing pattern is 6" on exterior lines and 8" down the middle line with 8d nails.

Windows are placed over sheathing.

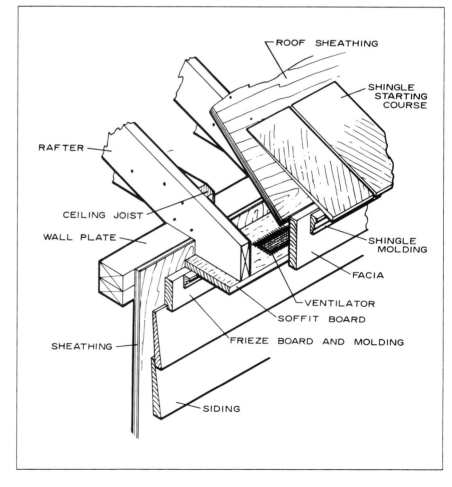

A narrow box cornice works well for covering undereaves. Don't eliminate the vents; either make cut-outs and install fiberglass screening for vents, or install commercial vents.

Siding is easier with two people, but it can be done with one. For slights, or aids, use a few $1'' \times 4''$ boards, pointed on one side of one end and notched on the other, to help support long siding pieces. An additional help is a little notched board, about twice as long as the siding is wide. The notch is cut into the board exactly the height of the part of the siding that is to be exposed to the weather (the exposure). Place the notched board on the already-in-place siding course, and use the top of the board to set the next piece, leaving the first piece perfect. This saves a lot of measuring.

Vertical board siding is also started in one corner, against a corner molding piece, if such molding is used (it need not be with most kinds of vertical siding). The board edge must be plumb, and you nail as indicated in the drawings. Board and batten is the most common kind of vertical siding, but there are also board and board, batten on board, and a couple of

Windows must be level and plumb in two planes.

Windows are then nailed through their flanges. Siding covers the flanges.

other ones. Shiplap is great, but it's a bit more costly.

Bring the siding on up to the eave line and cover the gable ends, and you're getting very close to occupying your shop.

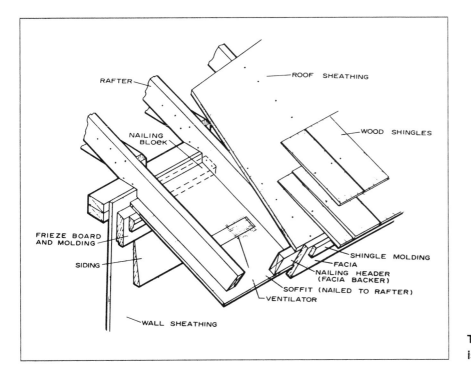

The wide box cornice, as shown here, is a possibility.

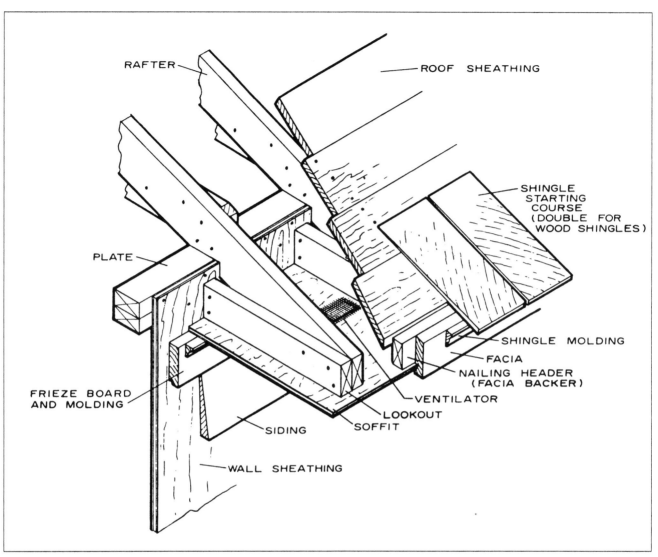

RAFTER

ROOF SHEATHING

SHINGLE
STARTING
COURSE
(DOUBLE FOR
WOOD SHINGLES)

PLATE

SHINGLE MOLDING

FACIA

NAILING HEADER
(FACIA BACKER)

FRIEZE BOARD
AND MOLDING

VENTILATOR

LOOKOUT

SOFFIT

SIDING

WALL SHEATHING

With look-outs, the wide box cornice is neater looking and easier to put up.

TRIM AND FINISH WORK

Trim work includes cornices, fascia and undereave soffit, along with the needed molding. You may also choose to leave your eave ends open. Where I live, that's too much of an invitation to starlings and stinging insects such as hornets and wasps.

For a true exterior finishing touch, you may want to add gutters, though they can be added later. The easiest gutters for the do-it-yourselfer to add are the snap-together vinyl types. Those all come with adequate instructions for installation, and most provide brochures that make selec-

tion of parts a simple matter. Without gutters, you need to spread gravel at least 4″ thick and 18″ wide as a splash area under each eave.

When the shop is all done, regardless of its size, start producing projects for your own enjoyment.

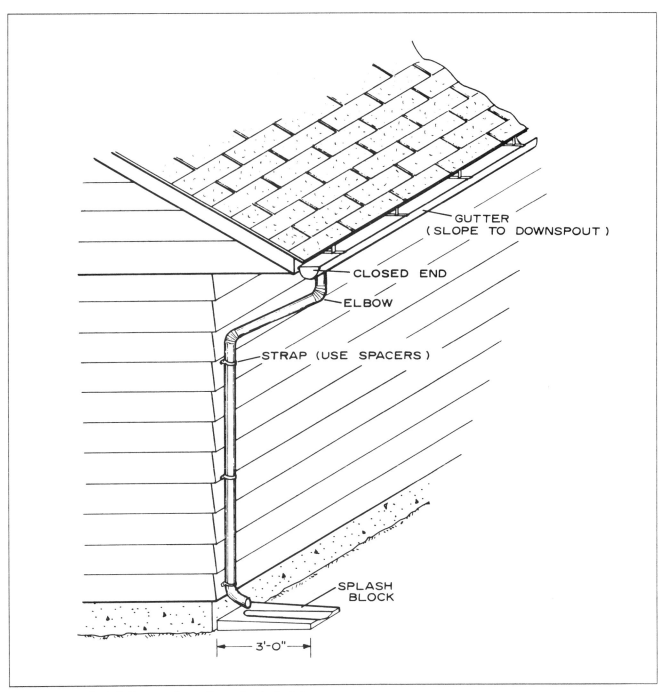

GUTTER
(SLOPE TO DOWNSPOUT)

CLOSED END

ELBOW

STRAP (USE SPACERS)

SPLASH
BLOCK

3'-0″

A basic gutter installation works well on simple buildings.

As the years pass, every wall in your shop will almost certainly be as full as this one.

INDEX

Other fine Betterway Books are available from your local bookstore or direct from the publisher. A complete catalog of Betterway Books is available FREE by writing to the address shown below, or by calling toll-free 1-800-289-0963. To order additional copies of this book, send in retail price of the book plus $3.50 postage and handling for one book, and $1.00 for each additional book. Ohio residents add 5½% sales tax. Allow 30 days for delivery.

Betterway Books
1507 Dana Avenue
Cincinnati, Ohio 45207

Stock is limited on some titles; prices subject to change without notice.